I0407463

Copyright © 2012 Samantha Tarplin.

samtarplin@live.co.uk

Contents

Acknowledgements

Some of the pictures in this book have been provided by the owners of **www.Basic-Horse-Care.com**, a website dedicated to offering free advice on looking after your horse. The website explores subjects such as showing and plaiting, exercising, stabling and grooming, buying a horse and how to look after your horse on snowy days. Visit their website for more information or to browse their shop.

A big thank you to you for helping me illustrate my explanations and sprucing the book up a bit!

Welcome! to your One Step Ahead Equine Studies Stable Management and Showing course.

This comprehensive study book has been put together for you to gain knowledge of the equine industry and to help give you a leg up onto your equine career ladder. The study provides essential information which is useful to have when working with horses and it will also look good from a potential employer's point of view if you already have a good understanding of the basics so they don't have to start training you from scratch. There is also a 'Going Further' section to this book where you can study in more depth, giving you a higher level of knowledge and understanding which can only help to improve your chances of impressing that future employer!

This study book is aimed towards people who already own a horse and want to know more or people intending to own a horse in the future but would like a better understanding of the animal beforehand. Students who are due to start or are already studying an equine course will also benefit from this wealth of information. This collection of material can be used to prepare you for college to give you a head start or used as a source of information to refer back to alongside the course.

With the freedom to study when it suits you and without the need to perform as you will not be assessed, there is no pressure on you so you can relax and enjoy your learning experience.

Complete the questions at the back either as you get to them or as you complete each topic to see how much you have remembered. There are questions for the 'Going Further' sections too if you fancy more of a challenge!

Whatever your reason for study, I hope you find this book to be straightforward and informative!

Stable Management

Typical Yard Duties

There are many different jobs that are undertaken on an equine yard and many of these tasks will vary according to how the employer prefers to run their yard and also in accordance with the type of horses kept there. Normally, there are certain tasks that are nearly always performed which you would be expected to do on any yard you go to. Different types of horses e.g. racing, riding school, rehabilitation cases will all require specialised routines and different types or levels of care. This is where the differences in routines really become apparent.

To the right is an example of a typical daily routine for a medium to large sized competition yard.

Time	Task
08:00	Feed horses
08:45	Turn horses out
09:15	Muck out stables
11:15	Hay round
11:30	Sweep yard
11:50	Tidy yard and put away tools
12:00	Lunch break
12:30	Bring horses in to be exercised
13:00	Exercise horses
14:15	Clean off tack
14:30	Bring in rest of horses
15:00	Pick up droppings from fields
15:30	Groom horses
16:00	Feed horses
16:15	Top up hay
16:30	Skip out stables
16:50	Sweep and tidy yard
17:00	Finished

Team Work

For all of these jobs to be completed efficiently and in a timely manner it is important that all yard staff work well together as a team. There should be someone in charge, usually a yard manager, who delegates the jobs and makes sure everything gets completed properly with minimal problems.

Sometimes problems can arise where people in a team may not work well together and this can cause friction within relationships and lead to jobs not being done properly or completed within an acceptable time scale. When problems like this occur it can lead to things being overlooked and the general upkeep of the yard can suffer so it is important to get these issues sorted out as quickly as possible. If you notice a problem like this then it should be brought up with the yard manager or whoever is in charge. Problems like this can usually be sorted out quickly if the issue is discussed with all who are involved and getting their input on what the issue is and how the situation can be improved. Sometimes, the implementation of team building exercises can really help bring a team of staff back together and improve their communication and work performance.

Mucking Out

Believe it or not there are actually a number of ways to muck out a stable. These different methods are used depending on the time of day and the time of year.

Figure 1: The daily muck out.

- **The daily full muck out** – This is the most common type of mucking out that is practised on most yards. It is normally done in the morning and requires all of the droppings and wet bedding to be removed **(Fig. 1)** with fresh bedding added if needed. This generally makes the stable look cleaner and tidier with fewer odours. This makes for a more professional appearance. As this provides a cleaner environment the horse is less likely to develop thrush as there are fewer bacteria under foot. It is also easier to monitor the horse's health, for example, a lack of droppings can indicate some serious health issues and the vet may need to be contacted for further investigation. Some downfalls to this type of mucking out are that there is more labour involved on a daily basis to keep the stable clean. It can also work out to be more expensive as bedding will need to be replaced every 1-2 days. Because the bedding is thinner and the floor is drier the horse is more likely to slip, especially if he has been shod. As the bedding is thinner it can also be less comfortable for the horse to lie down on. Rubber matting can be added to provide more comfort but this can be expensive to buy. This type of mucking out can be done all year round.

- **Skipping out** – This is a much briefer form of mucking out that requires only droppings to be removed and the bed swept back after the daily full muck out has been done. This is usually done whenever someone enters the stable to do something with the horse and at the end of the day. This helps to keep the horse clean and comfortable while he is stabled and also reduces the workload for the full muck out the following morning. It also helps to keep the stable looking clean and tidy which promotes a more professional appearance. This type of mucking out can be done all year round.

- **Deep litter** – This type of mucking out is less common but still widely used as it has its benefits. It involves removing all droppings but leaving in the wet bedding. The bed is then tidied up and fresh bedding is put on top. These beds are easier and quicker to maintain and are more cost effective as less bedding is used overall. Over time, the bed becomes thicker and warmer and can be useful to keep horses warm or to help cushion their feet if they are lame. This type of bed would not be suitable if the horse was lame due to an open wound or if heat would irritate the cause of the problem. Care must also be taken to keep the horse's feet in good condition. If they are not picked out regularly then the horse could develop thrush. The horse is also more likely to get dirty or get his rugs dirty. Some downfalls to this type of bed are that when the bedding is fully removed it is hard and unpleasant work. Also, once the bed is well established it can begin to look untidy and slopes can appear which can put uneven pressure on the horse's legs while he is standing in the stable. Because the wet bedding is left in the stable the smell can encourage the presence of flies and vermin which is something that will need to be monitored and kept on top of if it becomes a problem. This type of mucking out is used more during the winter for its warming benefits.

So How's It Done?

Mucking out is a fairly simple task and very soon becomes second nature. If you are mucking out your own horse then it is up to you how you go about the process. If you are mucking out for your employer then it is best to check beforehand if they have any preferences on how it is done. Below is a typical example of how to do a full muck out:

- If the horse is still in the stable he will need to be tied up with a head collar and lead rope. If there is a securing ring in his stable then he can be tied up in there and you can work around him or if he is fidgety and there are securing rings outside the stable then it might be easier to tie him up outside the stable.

- Collect your tools for mucking out. You will need a fork or shavings fork, shovel, broom and a wheel barrow.

- Remove any feed / water buckets and haynets if used.

- Using the fork, remove any droppings from the top of the bed.

- Fork through and turn over the banks (bedding that lines the walls) and remove any droppings.

- Put all clean bedding to one side or spread evenly on top of the banks.

- Remove any wet bedding and old hay.

- Using the broom, sweep the floor to collect any bits, dirty bedding and wetness and remove with the shovel.

- The bed can then either be left up for a bit to dry if the floor is quite wet or the bed can be put straight back down. This is more likely to be the case on a busier yard.

- To lay the bedding down use the fork to bring the bedding away from the walls (including the banks).

- Sweep by the walls to remove any dusty bits with the shovel.

- Lay the bed evenly over the stable floor and make sure that the bedding by the walls is higher to help prevent the horse rolling over and getting stuck up against the wall (this is called cast).

⅄ Add fresh bedding if any is needed and check the thickness of the bed by prodding it with the fork. If the fork easily goes through the bedding and hits the floor then it is too thin. If the fork feels cushioned then the bedding should be thick enough.

⅄ Sweep the front of the bed back so it is tidy then sweep up outside the stable.

⅄ Empty, scrub and rinse the water bucket then refill it and place it back in the stable.

⅄ Empty the wheel barrow onto the muck heap or into the muck trailer.

⅄ Remove all tools from the stable.

⅄ If the horse was tied up in the stable then untie him and remove the head collar and lead rope. If the horse was tied up outside the stable put him back in and remove the head collar and lead rope.

How to put on a head collar:

1. Make sure you have the correct head collar for that particular horse as sizes do vary.

2. Make sure the noseband is done up and the neck strap is undone.

3. Stand to the left of the horse facing forwards then slide the noseband of the head collar up the horse's nose with one hand on either side of the head collar.

4. Still standing to the left of the horse, take the neck strap in your right hand and gently fling it over the horse's neck so it is 1-2 inches behind the ears.

5. Fasten the neck strap so it is not too tight. You should be able to fit about 3 fingers between the strap and the horse.

6. Clip a lead rope onto the loose ring under the horse's jaw if you are going to lead or tie up the horse.

N.B. When tying a horse to a securing ring or any other solid object always attach some breakable string or twine with a loop to the ring or object first then tie the lead rope to the string or twine using a quick release knot. This allows the horse to break free if they panic. If the horse panics and cannot break free they can end up causing a lot of damage to themselves.

Disposing of Muck

There are a couple of ways to dispose of muck. One method is by creating a muck heap. This is pretty much what it sounds like. The muck is piled up in the same place and always added onto the top of the heap. Sometimes muck heaps can get big so it may be helpful to have a ramp up to the top of the heap so that the wheel barrow can be easily pushed to the top of the heap. When the heap is larger in size it is best to try to distribute the muck more evenly over the top so it is more spread out.

Figure 2: Forking back the muck trailer.

When using the muck heap method it is better to have three muck heaps. When the first one has got to the maximum size that your employer wishes to allow you can then begin to create the second heap. The first one should no longer be added to. When the second heap is at the maximum size the third heap can then be started on. Like the first, the second heap should now also not be added to. When the third muck heap is at its maximum size the first one should now have had enough time to decompose. This can now be used to spread on fields, bagged up and sold as compost or you can arrange to have it taken away. A new muck heap can be started in its place and the cycle can continue.

Another method to dispose of muck is to load it into a muck trailer **(Fig. 2)**. When the trailer is full you can arrange to have it taken away. The muck in the trailer is usually built up in steps, starting at the back, and trodden down to save as much space as possible.

Storage Buildings

You may find on a yard that there are a few different storage buildings and these are useful to have as there are various equine and yard related items that do benefit from proper storage. These storage buildings may include:

⋏ Feed room

⋏ Tack room

⋏ Tool shed

⋏ Hay / straw barn

Feed Room

Figure 3: A typical feed room with separate lidded bins for different feeds. Medicines and supplements are kept shelved away from damp and out of reach of children.

Most yards have a feed room **(Fig. 3)**. This is because the feed needs adequate storage to keep it clean, dry and away from vermin. Open bags of food are usually kept in feed bins. If the bag of food has been emptied into the bin then it is sensible to have the bin labelled so anyone preparing the feeds will know what is in that particular bin. The feed bin should have a lid kept on it at all times to prevent dust settling on the food and to prevent any unwanted visitors getting into the food.

Bags of feed that have not yet been opened should ideally be stored on top of pallets **(Fig. 4)**. This will keep the food dry as it is not touching the damp floor and it will also help to keep it out of reach of vermin. If there is evidence that something has chewed its way into a bag of feed then that bag of food should be discarded as it may have been contaminated with leptospirosis.

Figure 4: This is how feed bags should be stored.

For this reason, it is imperative that the feed room is thoroughly swept out on a daily basis because any food that drops onto the floor may encourage the presence of vermin.

Any medicines or supplements that are added to the feeds should be stored high up in a dry place away from the food and properly labelled.

Utensils that are used on a daily basis, such as scoops or stirring spoons, should be thoroughly washed off after each use. This is for hygiene purposes to prevent a build-up of bacteria and to keep the flies away. Also, any utensils have come into contact with a feed that has had medication or supplements added to it should be cleaned off before being used with another feed. This is to avoid contaminating another horse's feed – a horse that may be used for showing. If that horse shows up positive after a drugs test then he will not be allowed to enter the show.

Feed buckets should be scrubbed and washed out after each use to avoid a build-up of bacteria. Some horses are fussy and can refuse to eat out of a dirty feed bucket and who can blame them! This can then become costly as food is wasted.

Most feed rooms will have a feed chart somewhere on show which will list what each horse is given and at what times. If you are unsure of any information shown on a feed chart you should ask the person in charge for clarification because a sudden change in the horse's feed or feeding routine can cause digestive problems.

The feed room is normally located somewhere near the stables so it is quicker to get the feeds out to the horses. Some horses can get quite agitated or excited when they are expecting food so it is easier and safer to not keep them waiting for too long.

Below is an example of a feed chart:

Horse	Chaff	Mix	Pony Cubes	Sugar Beet	Medication
Cavalier	½ Scoop	1 Scoop	1 Scoop	1 Scoop	
Apollo	1 Scoop	2 Scoops	1 ½ Scoops	1 ½ Scoops	1 ACP Tablet
Monty	½ Scoop	1 ½ Scoops	1 Scoop	1 Scoop	
Tilly	¼ Scoop	½ Scoop	¼ Scoop	½ Scoop	
Indie	½ Scoop	1 Scoop	½ Scoop	1 Scoop	1 Sachet of Bute

Tack Room

Not all yards will have a tack room unless the horses there are used for riding or driving. However, a lot of yards do have one or at least a designated area for tack.

It is important to keep the tack off the floor to avoid it getting chewed by any rodents that may be around. To help

Figure 5: A good example of a well organised tack room with fittings for tack to sit on.

with this there is a handy wall fitting called a saddle rack that the saddle will sit on top of and the bridle can be hung underneath **(Fig. 5)**. These are quite common in many tack rooms.

The tack should be stored away tidily to prevent any tack getting mixed up or lost. This could be a particular problem on livery yards as the customers will store their tack together and will not want it going missing or getting damaged. The tack room should also be swept out regularly to keep up a professional appearance.

The location of the tack room is usually somewhere close to the stables as this prevents tack having to be carried long distances to the horses. This can make tacking up horses for riding lessons much quicker which is important at busy riding schools. At the end of the day the tack room should be well locked up and even better - alarmed. This is because it is an area of interest for thieves due to the value of tack.

Tool Shed

Most yards have a tool shed or a designated area for storing tools. It is important to keep this area as tidy as possible for safety reasons. An untidy tool area can lead to nasty accidents so it is best to be aware of your surroundings. Discipline yourself to put your tools away neatly and safely every time. Any tools that are hanging up should be facing the wall and any tools on the floor should be tucked away safely so as not to trip people up.

The tool area may need to be swept out every one to two days as tools can bring in bits of old bedding which will gather on the floor. One way to help prevent this from happening is to rinse off your tools after using them. This will help look after them and make them last longer.

The tool shed is normally kept near the stables. This just makes sense as it saves time if you find yourself going to and from the tool shed whilst mucking out.

Hay / Straw Barn

It is normal to have a designated area for hay and straw (or other types of bedding) and there is no reason why these cannot be stored together.

When collecting hay or bedding it is safer to only take what is near the ground level. If there is none that you can reach then rather than straining yourself or climbing bales ask for help. If the bales are stacked so high that they are not within reach then someone on the yard who is trained and licensed to drive a tractor will need to get them down.

It is useful every now and then to tidy up any loose hay or straw and if this is clean enough it can still be used. This can help save money as it makes the hay and straw last longer.

The location of this storage area should be well away from the stables. This is because hay and straw (and other beddings) burn quickly and easily. A fire could very quickly grow out of control and, if located nearby, spread to the stables. Building the storage area from materials such as breeze blocks or bricks may help to contain a fire if one were to break out **(Fig. 6)**.

Figure 6: Hay in a solid storage area built from breeze blocks.

Field Care

Shelter

If horses are being kept in a field they should have some form of shelter. If there is no natural form of shelter, such as trees or hedges, then it should be provided. Man-made field shelters are a bit like stables but are usually more open **(Fig. 7)**. Some people prefer to leave these shelters empty and will remove droppings whilst they are poo picking the rest of the field. This helps keep the work load to a minimum but it may be less comfortable for the horse and he may also get dirty if he decides to lie down in there. Other people prefer to put bedding in these shelters. This is comfy and drier for the horse but the work load increases as it becomes an extra stable to muck out. The bedding may also get wet if the rain is blown in which then can become a costly waste of supplies. This can also be cold and uncomfortable for the horse if he has to take shelter for some time.

These shelters will need to be checked regularly for safety as excitable horses passing by could easily catch themselves on something sharp and receive quite a nasty injury.

Figure 7: A typical open field shelter.

Figure 8: A tidily hung haynet that the horse cannot get caught up in.

Haynets can be hung up in the field shelter when the grass alone is not enough (**Fig. 8**). These will need to be removed once they are empty as a horse could get a foot tangled in it and get stuck. Water buckets can be kept in the shelter too. This way, everything is kept close together so it is quick and easy to check on everything and top things up. Water buckets can also be kept by the gate. This makes it easier and less tiring to fill up the buckets because it stops you having to carry water over long distances.

Water Supply

The water supply must be kept safe and clean. If it is kept in a bucket or a trough it should be cleaned out daily and refilled with clean, fresh water. If the water supply is a river a sample should be taken and tested to make sure it is safe for the horses to drink. Streams should be shallow, clean and without sand. The horses should not be able to access pond or canal water as this is stagnant and can be full of harmful pathogens.

Horses should have easy access to clean, fresh water at all times. Buckets may need to be filled up several times a day so they will need to be checked and refilled around 3 times a day (depending on the number of horses, how much water is given and how warm the weather is). If water is not readily available then the horse can become dehydrated and their condition could quickly deteriorate.

Field Cleanliness

Keeping the field clean is vital for the horse's health and safety. Clearing away objects helps to prevent accidents and removing droppings on a daily basis helps to prevent the horse from getting worms because the droppings contain worm eggs.

There are a couple of ways of going about removing droppings from a field. If it is a smaller field you may just need to go around with a bucket and a pair of rubber gloves and pick up the droppings. If the field is larger or there are a number of fields to clear then you may want to take a wheel barrow and a shavings fork or shovel as this will be quicker and easier. You can even get a field vacuum that has been made specifically for poo picking. All droppings that have been removed should be disposed of on the muck heap or muck trailer.

If the weather is quite warm and dry then the field can be harrowed which will break up and spread around the muck **(Fig. 9)**. This will then dry out and kill off any worm eggs. The field should be left empty for a couple of days to allow for this to happen so that the grass is safe to be grazed on again when horses are put back in there. Harrowing a field with droppings in it should not be done on a wet or cool day as this will not kill off the eggs, it will only spread them around the rest of the field. When the horse comes to graze on this grass they will then ingest the worm eggs which can lead to serious health issues.

Figure 9: Harrows that are pulled by a tractor or horses to rake the ground.

Field Safety

When horses are turned out into the field they can spend many hours unattended and they are free to run about and play however they please. For this reason it is so important to make sure the field is as safe as possible to help prevent injury. There are many hazards that can be found in the field so it is imperative that the field and its surroundings are checked regularly. You should look over the field as you take horses to and from it and the field should be thoroughly checked about once a week.

Things to look out for are:

- Broken fencing

- Nails / screws sticking out of fencing

- The gate opens and closes properly, staying securely in place when closed

- Gaps in the fencing for horses to escape through

- Holes in the ground

- Poisonous plants within the horse's reach

- Horses that have been separated because they do not get on cannot get to each other

- Rubbish in the field

- Items the horse could trip over, bump into or get tangled up in.

There are a number of plants that should be kept out of reach or removed if seen growing because, if ingested, they can make the horse ill or even cause death. These plants should be removed by the roots to prevent further growth and burned so they are destroyed without the risk of spreading seeds where they have been thrown away, causing more to grow.

Figure 10: Ragwort in flower (yellow). This plant is poisonous to horses.

A common plant that is found in many fields is ragwort **(Fig. 10)**. This is poisonous to horses if it is consumed in large quantities or over a long period of time. The vet should be called if it is thought that a horse has been eating ragwort so that treatment can be given before too much harm is caused.

Winter Care

Rugging Up

Winter can be a harsh time for horses, especially if they are old or their breed has thin skin and hair such as thoroughbreds. Care and consideration will need to be taken when turning horses out as some horses will need rugging up well and some might not need it at all **(Fig. 11)**. Some horses may only need a rug on when turned out but some will need rugging up in their stables too. Again, this depends on the breed, age and how warm and draught free the stable is.

Figure 11: These horses have been suitably rugged up according to the weather. Extras can be added to the rug to help provide even more coverage and warmth as seen on this horse's neck.

How to put on and remove a rug:

1. Fold the rug in half so the underneath of the rug is on the outside and the neck and tail end of the rug meet.

2. Place the rug over the horse so the neck of the rug is well

above the horse's withers. Avoid pulling the rug upwards as this pulls the hairs back and becomes uncomfortable. Place the rug higher up the neck to begin with if needs be.

3. Unfold the rug so it now covers the whole of the horse's body.

4. Cross the surcingles under the horse and fasten them to the opposite side of the rug. Fastening these first means the majority of the rug is held onto the horse if they bolt. It is less likely to slip to the front or rear of the horse causing a fall.

5. Fasten the chest straps so the rug is roomy at the front to allow the horse freedom to move around and graze.

6. Fasten the leg straps by passing one strap between the hind legs and fastening it to the loop on the same side of the rug further back. Repeat for the leg strap on the other side but as you pass the strap between the hind legs thread it through the leg strap on the other side first. This helps to prevent rubbing.

7. To remove – Undo leg straps and fasten to the loop on the same side without going through the legs. Next, undo the chest straps then surcingles and pull the rug off in one swift movement from front to back.

If horses are living out and rugged up their body condition needs to be checked a couple of times per week to make sure they are keeping their weight up. A rug can mask a horse's body condition as it will cover up signs of weight loss and other problems such as lumps, skin conditions and even injuries. Rugs also need to be checked on a daily basis for damage and loose or undone straps or buckles to prevent any accidents. They should also be checked for moisture as a cold, damp rug will not be able to do its job – particularly on a cold day.

Freezing Water

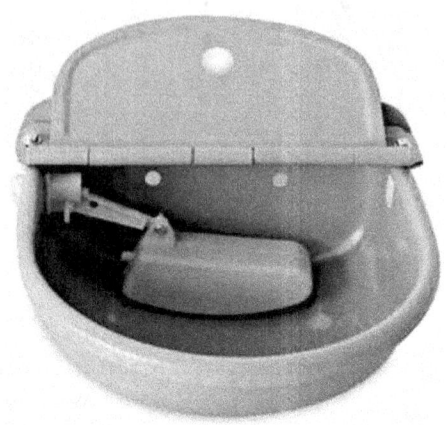

Any water supply that the horse has should be checked regularly as cold weather can cause it to freeze over, leaving the horse without water. If there are automatic drinkers **(Fig. 12)** in the stables the water may freeze in the pipes so when the bowl of water becomes low it will fail to refill itself. If this is the case you will have to provide the horses with buckets of water so they don't go without. Also, if you know

Figure 12: An automatic drinker showing the float that causes the bowl to fill when it lowers with the water level.

it is going to be a particularly cold night then it may be a good idea to leave a bucket of water in the stable just in case the pipes do freeze and the horse cannot get to any water over night. Be aware that when frozen pipes thaw out they can sometimes burst and flood out the stable! If the water buckets freeze up try putting a ball or some apples in the water to help keep the ice away. The horse may try to play with them and the movement will help stop the water from freezing over. This method may only be a temporary fix because the horse will rest overnight giving the water chance to freeze over. Placing the bucket in an old tyre and packing straw in around it may help to insulate the bucket and may prevent or delay the appearance of ice. Even if you have a method that seems to keep the ice away it is still a good idea to check the water regularly and break any ice that may have formed. Adding warm (not hot) water may also delay the appearance of ice.

Winter Feeding

In general, it costs more to feed horses over the winter as they need more body fat to help keep them warm. In addition, they will need more hay as the grass will be of poor quality and will not grow back as quickly as it does during the warmer months. Hay will need to be given in the field if the grass is in short supply. If there are a number of horses in the field then making several well-spaced out piles of hay will help to prevent the horses fighting and each horse will have a chance to get their share of hay.

Competition horses will need to have their feeds carefully adjusted to make sure they are still receiving all of the nutrition and energy they need to help keep them fit and warm but without causing them to put on too much weight as they need to be in tip top condition for competing.

Horses that are kept for leisure are okay to carry a little more fat over the winter to help keep them warm providing they have no medical conditions that can be affected by their diet or weight. Foods such as flaked maize or cooked barley can be increased or added to the horse's feed to help provide that little bit more fat. Monitor the horse's body condition once you have increased the feed to make sure you are not over-feeding. Any changes that are made to the feed should be done gradually over the course of one to two weeks depending on how big the change is. If you are introducing a new feed then only a small amount should be given at first and slowly increased over a four week period. This allows time for the horse's gut to get used to the food and produce the flora and enzymes needed to break the new feed down. Introducing a new feed too quickly can cause colic which is a big killer in horses.

When feeding horses in the field you must be very aware of the horses around you and you should be quick and calm in your approach to hand out the feeds. Feeding time can be very exciting for horses and they can start racing around, fighting and even get boisterous towards the person handing out the feeds. If you are not confident about this task then it is best to ask for help as it could be dangerous if you do not do it properly.

Feeding one horse on its own in a field is much easier. You should enter the field, securely closing the gate behind you then place the feed bowl on the floor near to the gate as you have less distance to travel carrying food with an excitable horse following you. It is also easier for you to collect the bowl afterwards as you do not have to walk far to get it.

When feeding a group of horses in a field you should enter the field confidently, securing the gate behind you. Drop a feed bowl on the floor for each horse with a good distance between each one to help prevent fights breaking out. Be careful not to get in between the group of horses while feeding as you could easily get kicked. Be prepared to see some horses putting their ears back, pulling threatening faces and trying to bite or kick each other. This can happen because they are excited about feed time and they are trying to keep their place in the herd's hierarchy. Once all of the feed bowls have been given out you should exit the field and come back to collect the bowls when all of the horses have finished eating. If you are not confident feeding a group of horses in the field and no one is available to help you then you can drop the feed bowls over the fence instead. This should be done quickly with a good space in between each bowl. If a horse requires a different feed to the other horses, needs their diet closely monitoring or needs medication with their feed then they should always be taken out of the field beforehand and fed on their own. They can be returned to the field when the other horses have finished their feeds and the bowls have been collected.

The Grass Kept Horse

Field Checks

When horses are living out it is important to check them and their surroundings on a daily basis. This is because things can easily go wrong and hay or water supplies will need topping up. The daily checking should include:

- ⅄ Field safety.

- ⅄ Water buckets should have plenty of water in them and topped up when needed. Break ice if it is cold.

- ⅄ If hay is given in winter there should be plenty available for grazing on.

- ⅄ Ensure there is adequate shelter and shade. This may be a problem in winter if trees were providing shelter but they are now bare. In this case horses may need to be brought

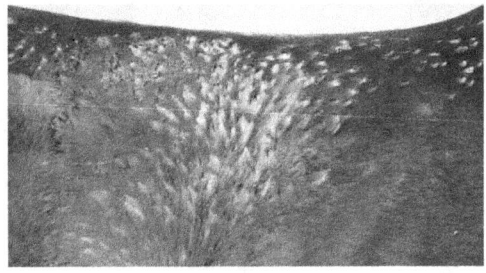

Figure 13: An example of rain scald, also known as rain rot.

in if it rains or snows. If there is not enough shade in the summer then the horses should be brought in during the hottest part of the day and offered plenty of water whilst turned out.

- ⅄ Check horse's ears for mites.

- ⅄ Apply fly repellent if flies are present (mainly around summer time).

⅄ Check for rain scald (scabs and hair loss on the dorsal aspect – upper part of the horse) **(Fig. 13)**.

⅄ Check for mud fever **(Fig. 14)** and abrasions on the horse's heels.

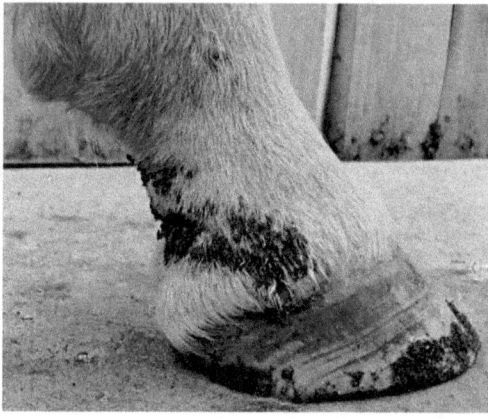

Figure 14: An example of mud fever on the heel.

⅄ The horse's rug should fit properly and provide adequate warmth without rubbing. It should be lying in the right position on the horse.

⅄ Look under the horse's rug to check their body condition. They should not be skinny and their skin should quickly lie flat after being gently pinched. The hair should be shiny, not dull or patchy. Check for any injuries such as broken skin, bumps, tenderness or limping.

⅄ Pick the horse's feet out.

Turning Out / Bringing In

If the horses are being brought in during the week for exercise and turned back out afterwards then use this time to give them a groom to remove any mud or dirt to help keep the horse comfortable and looking presentable. If the horses are not really brought in and used during the week then bring them in once a week for a good groom. If it is warm enough maybe even give them a bath to keep them clean and comfortable. This can also help to bond a person with their horse.

How to turn out a horse:

1. Lead the horse to the field with a head collar or chifney (if the horse pulls or rears) and lead rope.

2. Open the gate and enter the field with the horse, closing the gate behind you.

3. Turn the horse to face the gate squarely.

4. Undo and remove the head collar then step back out of the way in case the horse decides to turn and charge off.

5. If there is more than one person in the field about to release a horse follow all of the steps above then one person should count to 3 and all of the horses should be released at the same time.

6. Exit the field and securely close the gate behind you.

How to bring in a horse:

1. If the horse or horses are far off try to gain their attention by calling them or rattling a feed bucket.

2. When the horse is near to the gate enter the field and secure the gate behind you.

3. Approach the horse from the front or to the side, never from behind.

4. Put on the head collar or chifney with a lead rope already attached to it then lead the horse out of the field and secure the gate closed behind you.

5. If there are multiple horses in the field try to avoid leaving one horse in the field alone. Doing so can cause the horse to become worked up because they want to follow the herd. This can also make them difficult to bring in.

Figure 15: Leading a horse in from the field wearing the correct PPE.

Lead the horse by standing to the left at their shoulder. Hold the lead rope with your right hand 2 – 3 hand widths down from the horse's head. Hold the other end of the lead rope with your left hand to prevent any rope dangling down **(Fig 15)**. Without turning to face the horse ask them to walk on then take a positive step forward. If the horse refuses to walk after a couple of attempts a gentle tap to the horse's side or rump with the end of the lead rope can help. Bring the horse to halt by saying "and woahhh".

Feeding

We feed horses to provide them with the essential vitamins and nutrients their bodies need for their bodily systems to work properly and so they have adequate energy to cope with the exercise we require them to do. It also gives them a layer of fat to help keep them warm. Knowing what to feed a horse can be a little daunting so it is best to break it down to make it easier for working out what should be fed and in what quantities.

Figure 16: Concentrates.

Types Of Feed

Figure 17: Roughage.

There is a wide range of equine feeds on the market. To make it simpler these are concentrates **(Fig. 16)**, roughage **(Fig. 17)** or succulents **(Fig 18)** and they are made up of seeds, stalks, roots or fruit. Concentrates are the hard ingredients you would mix into a bucket to feed the horse. This, for example, could be hard pellets or mix which are normally made up of different seeds. Roughage is mainly grass and hay. It is the stalks that the

Figure 18: Succulents and roots.

horse eats and they will sometimes even eat straw bedding given half the chance. Succulents are food with plenty of moisture such as apples, carrots and soaked sugar beet. Carrots and sugar beet are also classed as root foods because they are grown straight from the roots rather than off a plant. And finally, fruit such as apples make a tasty treat.

How To Feed

Feeds and quantities for each horse are usually written down in a table so it is easy to see what each one is meant to have. There should be one scoop for each different feed to help prevent different foodstuffs getting mixed up together. Using the correct sized scoop, start adding the feed to the horse's bowl. Once you

Figure 19: A swivel manger.

have finished give the feed a quick stir so the horse cannot pick at its favourite bits and leave other bits out. If medication needs to be added to a feed make sure beforehand you know exactly what and how much the horse needs and this must be put in the correct bowl so the right horse receives their medication. Getting this wrong can be dangerous for a horse that has missed a dose or a horse that has received a dose of something they shouldn't have had. The medication should be mixed into the feed with a separate spoon which should then be washed off straight away before touching any other feed. This is to prevent contaminating another horse's feed with the medicine. Once all of the feeds have been prepared they should be given out preferably in order of the horses that are closer to you to prevent them getting wound up by seeing food go by. If the horses are being fed in the field then do this as described on page. If horses are being fed in their stables you should place the feed either inside on the floor by the door or in the manger if these are used. Placing the food inside by the door is safer as you do not have to walk into a stable with an excited horse – this is obviously safer! Some stables have a manger whereby you have to enter the stable to get to it. You should do this confidently and swiftly to prevent the horse getting wound up if they are excitable. You should also close and secure the stable door as you enter and exit the stable to prevent any escapes! Some mangers are on the outer wall of the stable and can be filled up from outside the stable then rotated so the manger is inside the stable for the horse to get to **(Fig. 19)**. This is a safer method of feeding as you do not have to enter the stable at all.

Once the horses have finished eating you should then remove the feed bowls and thoroughly wash them out. The same should be done with rotatable mangers. An ideal time to clean mangers inside the stable is while you are mucking out. This way the horse is either out of the stable or already tied up.

Hay

A horse's diet requires a large amount of roughage. Horses turned out to graze have the freedom to eat as much grass as they like. This is good because grass is a succulent source of roughage. Horses living in should be given plenty of roughage throughout the day and last thing at night. This is so they can receive the fibre they would get if they were out grazing all day. The horse's digestive system is designed to receive food little

Figure 20: A typical hay rack.

and often so they should have roughage available to them at all times. Horses that are turned out in the day and stabled at night should have roughage available to them in the stable. This should be topped up at night. If during the winter the grass is poor hay should be put out in piles so the horses can still graze.

A horse needs to eat 2.5% of its bodyweight in food per day and at least 65% of this should be roughage depending on the level of physical work they do each day.

Figure 21: Weighing a haynet using a spring balance.

Hay can be given to the horse either on the stable floor (which is a more natural position for the horse to eat), from a hay rack **(Fig. 20)** (which is easy to fill but can cause dust to fall into the horse's eyes) or from a hay net **(Fig. 8)** (which can be awkward to fill and dangerous if left empty in a stable but great for accurately weighing out hay with the help of a spring balance) **(Fig. 21)**.

Before dishing out hay it should be gently shook to help any dust or bits to fall out, making it more pleasant for the horse to eat.

If a horse requires a low sugar diet or has dust allergies the hay should be soaked in clean, fresh water beforehand for about 10 minutes then allowed to drain thoroughly before being given. Horses that require higher levels of energy may be given haylage. This is hay that has been wrapped up and slightly fermented and so contains more moisture and sugar making it high in energy. You can tell the difference between hay and haylage by the aroma. Haylage is sweeter smelling and more moist than normal hay.

Water

It is imperative that water is always available to the horse whether they are stabled or turned out. Without water, a horse can quickly become dehydrated. A horse cannot survive without water and if they go without then their condition can quickly deteriorate. Water also helps move food through the digestive system and therefore helps to prevent colic. Their water should be clean, fresh and readily available.

Cleanliness

It is good practice to keep things clean as you go along to keep everything hygienic. If utensils and bowls are left unclean food can become encrusted on them. This can cause bacteria and encourage flies which can lead to maggots. Keep utensils clean and safe by rinsing them off after preparing feeds. Feed bowls should be kept clean for the same reason. Anything that has come into contact with medication should be cleaned thoroughly straight away to prevent contamination to other feeds and horses. The feed room should be swept out at least once a day and the floor disinfected, rinsed and thoroughly swept out once a week to remove any feed residue. This is to reduce the risk of vermin appearing.

<u>Going Further</u>

The Stable

Sizing It Up

It is important that a horse is kept in a stable that is the right size for them. Too small and the horse is more likely to bump themselves. They may not have room to lie down safely without getting cast, they may struggle to move around and they may become stressed or frustrated due to their lack of space. If the horse is given too much room they may be more likely to pace around the stable if they get bored. This can lead to a waste of energy which is not favourable for competition horses. It also means there is a larger area to muck out which takes longer, is harder work and costs more in bedding. Ideally the horse should have enough room to roll without getting stuck.

The following measurements below are a guide as to what size stable horses should have for them to be most comfortable in:

Size of Horse	Size of Stable	
Ponies and up to 15hh	10' X 10'	(3.0m X 3.0m)
Horses above 15hh	12' X 12'	(3.6m X 3.6m)
Large or heavy horses	12' X 14'	(3.6m X 4.2m)
Foaling box	12' X 16'	(3.6m X 4.8m)
Other Measurements		
Kick boards	4' (1.2m) high	
Height up to eaves	7' (2.1m) high	
Bottom door	4' (1.2m) high	
Top door	3' (0.9m) high	
Door width	4' (1.2m) wide	

Ventilation vs Temperature

Plenty of ventilation is the key to maintaining fresh, airy stables. Muggy, odorous air will make a horse grumpy and uncomfortable. The best way to get plenty of fresh air in is to leave the top stable door open at all times if possible. Having a window in the back wall will also allow air to flow through the stable but this should be carefully placed as you don't want there to be a draught which could make the horse cold. Louvered boards will allow fresh air to come into the stable and flow upwards. Gaps in the tiles on the roof of the stable will allow hot, stale air to escape from the stable. This should all help to make a stable feel and smell fresher and more airy.

Getting the ventilation right will help with the control of the temperature. A hot or cold environment will be uncomfortable which can lead to a moody, difficult horse. Stables built of tin or corrugated iron become very hot in the summer as the sun warms the metal up until it becomes hot. The atmosphere inside the stable becomes stuffy and odorous as the air is hot which causes the bedding to smell more. In the winter the metal becomes very cold and therefore provides no warmth whatsoever for the horse making the stable very cold to live in.

Whereas a brick built stable is more expensive, it is worth it in the long run as the building is stronger and the temperature is easier to regulate. This is because brick offers good insulation. It is warmer for the horse in the winter and cooler for the horse in the summer.

The height of the roof can also influence the temperature of the stable. This is because of the amount of room that the air has to circulate. If the roof is low there is less room for air to circulate so the air becomes hotter. A tall roof offers plenty of room for circulation so the air becomes cooler.

Stable Layout

Below is a diagram of a typical layout of a stable. All fittings and accessories are labelled and placed where they would be safe and convenient:

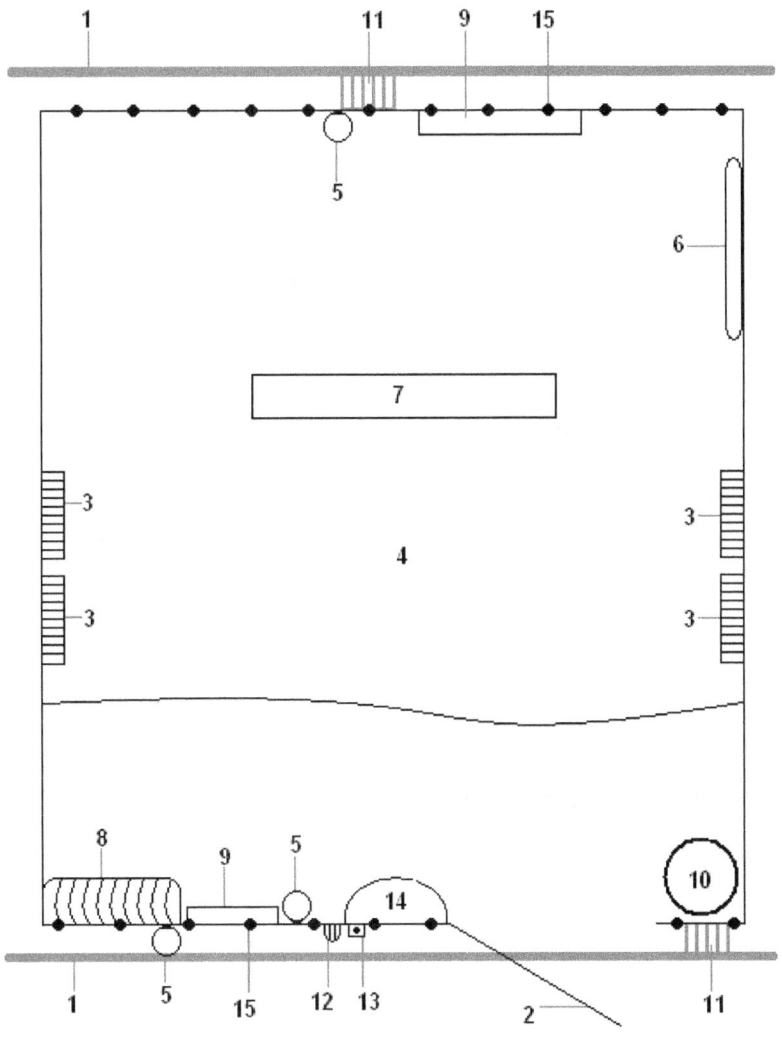

Key

1. Gutter

2. Stable door

3. Barred holes in the wall which act as windows

4. Bedding

5. Tie rings

6. Rug rack

7. Strip lighting with plastic covering

8. Hay rack or ring for haynets

9. Window (hole in wall)

10. Water bowl

11. Drain

12. Weather proof outside light

13. Weather proof light switch

14. Feed bucket or manger

15. Drainage holes

Stable Accessories

You may notice that most of the stable accessories are at the front of the stable. This is for safe, easy access to them as they need to be filled or used regularly.

The flooring of the stable should ideally be made of concrete. This is because it is easy to keep clean and is less likely to harbour germs like a soft earthen floor will. The floor should be at a very slight angle, sloping down towards the back of the stable. This is so that any urine or water can naturally run down and drain out through the drainage holes which lead to the gutter and drain. Drainage holes should be cleared out regularly as they can easily become blocked with bedding and then fail to do their job. Drains should also regularly be cleared of any bedding as this will block them up and there will be nowhere for water or urine to go.

Windows at the front and rear of the stable allow the horse to look around and see their friends. It gives more of a feeling of freedom and with more to look at the horse is less likely to become bored and develop stable vices (repetitive boredom breaking actions). Windows to both sides of the stable allows the horse to see their next door neighbour which can help them feel settled and less isolated or cooped up. The bars are there to stop the horses from trying to get to each other and to help prevent biting.

The rug rack is in the corner of the stable as it is out of the way and the rugs are less likely to get tripped over. If the horse has a tendency to play with the rug or gets the rug dirty while it is in there you could move the rug rack to the outside of the front wall of the stable. This should only be done if the stable is inside and not exposed to the elements.

Any outdoor lights or switches should be kept out of reach of the horse as the electrics will be dangerous if the horse decides to play with them!

Figure 22: An overhang that shelters the horses and staff.

Outdoor stables should have an overhang **(Fig. 22)** to help shelter
the horses if their heads are over the stable doors and to help
prevent driving rain from getting into the stables. If horses are
hanging their heads out on a hot day you may need to put sun
cream on their noses to stop them getting burned. Overhangs also
help to shelter staff who are going from stable to stable doing
duties. Correct work attire such as waterproof clothing or summer
wear (a hat and light clothing covering skin to prevent burning)
will also help keep staff dry or sheltered from the sun.

Bedding

There is a wide variety of bedding used today and they are used in stables, stalls, horse boxes and trailers. Bedding is used for a number of reasons. It is more comfortable for the horse, not only to lie down on but to stand on too. Horses also dislike passing urine on hard surfaces as it can splash their legs and bedding helps to prevent this so it encourages the horse to urinate. When the urine is absorbed into the bedding some of the smell of ammonia is absorbed as well so the overall smell is reduced. Bedding also gives the horse more stability under foot, especially on concrete floors. Beware though, clean, fresh straw on smooth floors can add to slipperiness so it may not be the best bedding to use in a horse box or trailer.

Bedding provides warmth as it prevents the horse from coming into direct contact with the cold floor and it also helps to block draughts. The cushioning effect of bedding helps to prevent injuries and sores when the horse lies down and gets up. Using bedding to create banks will also help to prevent the horse getting cast.

Types of Bedding

Straw (Fig. 23) is probably the most common bedding used on yards because it is usually cheap and easy to get hold of (depending on how good the harvest was). There are three different types of straw that can be used; oat, barley and wheat. The horse will quite happily eat all three of these types of straw so it is best to make sure hay is always available! Barley straw can also have sharp awns which

Figure 23: Straw.

can irritate the horse skin. Like with hay, straw has dust and spores that can cause coughing and allergic reactions so it is not suitable for all horses.

When it comes to mucking out, a straw bed can be heavy but it is easy to dispose of. Once bedding has been replaced, the stable looks bright and fresh.

Shavings (Fig. 24) are also quite commonly used on yards. It is more expensive to buy than straw but it does have some benefits. A shavings bed is quick and easy to muck out, which is always a bonus on busy yards. The dust has usually been extracted from the shavings before being baled up so it is better for horses that are more

Figure 24: Shavings.

sensitive to dust and mould spores. A fresh bed looks bright, clean and tidy and less shavings are needed as they offer substantial padding and are less likely to get eaten! A soiled bed is also lighter to work with which makes the work load lighter.

On the down side, it can be harder to dispose of dirty shavings. They can be burned but this depends on if there are houses nearby. Some people may not appreciate a burning muck heap near their property. It may be wise to ask your neighbours beforehand if they are happy with you doing this to prevent any complaints or upsets. After a couple of days a shavings bed, although having been cleaned out, may still look dirty.

If a horse has an open wound and is being kept stabled shavings should not be used as they will stick to the wound and can cause irritation and infection. Sharper shavings may irritate the horse's heels and can even discourage them to stand on the bedding.

Hemp (Fig. 25) is a plant that is not used quite so widely as straw or shavings. It is a similar price to good quality shavings so it is not particularly cheap. It is very absorbent and therefore makes good bedding for deep litter. It is dust free bedding so it is good for allergy prone horses and it is also

Figure 25: Hemp.

unpalatable so it is good for horses that have a tendency to graze on their bedding. This is a quick and easy bedding to muck out as wet areas do not need to be removed as frequently due to its absorbency. Regular topping up keeps the bed fresh.

Shredded paper (Fig. 26) can be cheap or even free if you know of an office or somewhere that regularly shreds paper. You can even shred your own newspapers to use for bedding. Once shredded, paper can fluff up quite well and is dust and spore free. You must, however, make sure there are no sharp objects in the paper such as

Figure 26: Shredded Paper.

staples or paper clips as these can be sharp for the horse and cause injury.

This is an easy bedding to dispose of because it will rot down quickly and so can be turned into a muck heap and used on gardens. It can also be easily burned once it has dried out (providing neighbours are happy with this!).

There are a couple of down sides to using paper bedding. It looks messy and unprofessional so it is probably not suitable for yards that are used for business. If newspaper is used it can very quickly make lighter coloured horses look dirty. In some cases the printers ink can even irritate the horse's skin. Also, as this bedding is used on fewer yards, muck collectors may be less willing to collect it so you will need to be able to make sure you can dispose of it yourself via burning or composting.

Rubber matting (Fig. 27) is very expensive flooring for a stable but it provides steady footing, warmth, comfort and less bedding is needed on top. It should cover the whole floor of the stable to prevent tripping. If bedding is not used on top of the matting the horse can become uncomfortable and cold and they are less likely to urinate as they will not want to splash their legs. They can also get really dirty quite quickly as there is nothing to help drain and absorb the urine.

Providing the stable is not on deep litter the mats will need to be disinfected approximately once a month. If the mats do not join properly or do not meet the walls properly they will need to be taken out every now and then to remove any build-up of waste in between the gaps. The matting will also need to be thoroughly disinfected once taken off deep litter.

Figure 27: Rubber matting.

Environmental Considerations

When a yard is built there are many things that need to be
carefully considered beforehand regarding placement of
buildings, what they will look like, noise, smell, disposal of muck
etc. There is quite a lot to think about and some things that may
only seem like minor problems could actually become quite a
stumbling block.

Planning Permission

Firstly you need that all important planning permission. Without
this you cannot go ahead and build. To get permission you will
need to prepare your plans of the site location and a layout of the
yard complete with measurements. There are many factors that
can affect whether you are granted permission to build or not but
there are some things you can do to help your case. The yard
should fit in with its environment and be aesthetically pleasing.
For example, a big concrete building in a picturesque village set
in the countryside may not go down too well. The area to be built
on should be plenty big enough and the buildings should not be
too close to the borders.

Once the plans have been drawn up they should be submitted to
the local planning authority – part of the local council. It can take
around 8 weeks to hear back.

Materials

Some things to take into consideration with the construction of
the yard are what materials are going to be used. Baring in mind
the hard work that needs to be done on a yard on a day to day
basis you may want to layout the yard so that it is going to be low
maintenance. Things such as poured concrete flooring in areas
where bedding may need sweeping up regularly will help with
tidying up times. Having a gutter and drains that are easy to
access will prove invaluable at times of heavy rainfall.

Figure 28: An example of reforestation.

To help keep costs down you can try sourcing your materials from
local suppliers. Their prices may be cheaper and this also helps
the economy by helping smaller businesses. If you are building
your stables out of wood you may want to consider helping the
environment by buying wood from suppliers that have planted
trees in place of those cut down **(Fig. 28)**.

Neighbours

It is very important to always consider your neighbours when
building and running the yard. While building the yard you may
want to let neighbours know if you are going to be doing any
particularly noisy work. This is just courteous and they will
probably appreciate it as they can plan around it. It also helps to
establish a good relationship with the people nearby which is
much better than getting off on the wrong foot!

Things to consider are:

⅄ The appearance of your yard

   ⅄ It should be tidy and preferably attractive.

⅄ It should not overshadow their property or cut out their light.

⅄ Noise levels

   ⅄ Machinery should not be used at night when families are in and may want some peace after a long day!

   ⅄ Busy periods where people come to the yard (such as on riding yards) should be kept to daytimes. Vehicles coming and going can produce road noise which people may not want to hear when they live in the country. People tend to live there for a quieter life!

   ⅄ If the horses tend to be noisy and whinny a lot then you may want to build the stables away from any housing, facing them away if possible.

   ⅄ Farriers can also be noisy when hammering shoes so daytime visits are better.

⅄ Smell

   ⅄ Muck heaps or trailers should be kept well away from neighbouring properties. They are not going to want to sit in their back garden with the smell of horse manure lingering in the air accompanied by a large number of flies. The trailer or muck heap should ideally be kept out of view of the neighbours if possible as it is not a pleasant thing for them to have to look at. If there is nowhere adequate to hide it then you could always consider building a brick wall around the muck storage area. This can also help to prevent muck heaps getting too big and therefore helps to reduce mess. Trailers should be emptied regularly and muck heaps carefully maintained to help keep the smell down. These should not be kept too close to the stables as flies will gather and the horses won't appreciate the smell or the flies.

If you keep a good level of hygiene in all aspects of the yard there is less chance of any odours and the yard will be a more pleasant environment to  work in. This will also lower the chance of vermin making an appearance. Neighbours won't be happy if they have rats running around their property and find they have come from your yard! Workers will be happier in a cleaner environment, as will the horses and it is less likely that staff or animals will become ill from unhygienic conditions.

Energy Efficiency

Making the yard energy efficient can really help with keeping the outgoings down and it is better for the environment too.

A good place to start is energy consumption. Cutting down on what is used can really save a lot of money. Turning lights off when they are not needed, turning taps off instead of leaving them running, using low wattage energy efficient light bulbs **(Fig. 29)** where possible, refraining from repeatedly reheating the kettle at break times and not putting more water in the kettle than is needed can all help to cut down those bills! Using reusable energy can also be cheaper in the long run. Solar panels on the stable roof could power the internal and external lights. You could even have a little wind turbine to create power for your yard. Any leftover energy can be sold to the national grid so not only are you saving money but a little profit can be made too! If the ground is right for it then a well or a water pump could be used so you do not need to pay for a water supply. Rain water could be stored in water butts and used to wash buckets or soak hay nets.

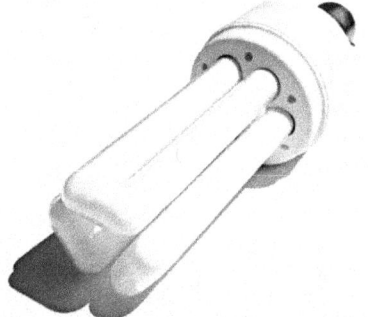

Figure 29: A typical energy saving light bulb.

Turning off vehicles that are not in use such as tractors and horse boxes etc. will also help you save fuel which is becoming increasingly more expensive. This will help the environment too as there will be less pollution.

To help save materials in the winter and to create a warmer environment for the horses you could consider putting your horses on deep litter. This is warmer for them which is ideal for the time of year and less bedding is used too so it works out to be cheaper.

Field Care

Fencing

As a general rule there should be one acre of land available for each horse. So five horses would require five acres. A pony can get by fine with half an acre. During the winter you may need to double the land available to them because of the quality of the grass. If this is not a viable option then feeding additional hay in the field **(Fig. 30)** is a must or else the horse will simply just not be able to find enough roughage while they are turned out.

Figure 30: These horses have been given hay because the wintry conditions are preventing them from grazing grass.

Figure 31: A post and rail fence.

There should be a strong, sturdy fence around the field to stop the horses escaping and it should be able to withstand bumps and kicks. A post and rail fence **(Fig. 31)** is the most common as this is a safe and sturdy structure. Make sure there are no nails protruding as this will be extremely dangerous for the horses.

Electric fencing **(Fig. 32)** is good if you cannot afford a well-built wooden fence. The live wire will keep horses away from the fence, will stop intruders getting to the horses and can also be good for sectioning off a field into smaller areas.

Hedging can be used as a barrier to keep horses in a field but it may be wise to have some form of fencing there too as during the

Figure 32: An electric tape and stake fence.

winter the hedge may look a bit bare and the horses may try to make a break for it. Seeing a fence in the way too may help put them off the idea. Hawthorne is a good type of hedging to use as it is dense and is not poisonous to horses. Stone walls **(Fig. 33)** are another option to keep your horses in. They are strong and the horse cannot see what is on the other side which may discourage a horse from attempting to jump it if they have a tendency to do this.

Figure 33: A stone wall offers a strong, sturdy border to a field.

Barbed wire **(Fig. 34)** should never be used. While it will put people off climbing onto your land it can be a huge risk to the safety of the horse. Skin can easily get lacerated and the vet bills will become pricey! Similarly, looped wire should not be used either. It may look like a barrier to the horse but they could quite easily get tangled up in it. Once a horse panics they thrash around and try to escape and this could just make matters worse.

Figure 34: Horses can get stuck in barbed wire fencing causing large, devastating injuries.

Mesh fencing (**Fig. 35**) should also not be used. It is ideal for smaller animals such as chickens or sheep but it is not strong enough for horses and will not act as much of a barrier. It could even be difficult to see!

Gates into the field should ideally be a metal cross rail gate. These are strong, heavy and do the job well. They should swing freely when opened without hanging off the hinges or dragging on the ground. Keep an eye out for rust on older gates. This can be sharp and can become dangerous to people using the gate or to the horse who may pace up and down by the gate when they know it is time to come in. Ideally, when the gate starts to deteriorate it should be replaced before it becomes a danger.

Figure 35: Mesh Fencing is not strong enough for horses. They can also get their feet caught in it.

Gateways should be looked after, particularly when it rains a lot. These areas can get quite muddy because the horses pass through here and stand or pace up and down at the gate. This can make it difficult for people to get in or out of the field which is dangerous when trying to lead a horse. Deep mud can suck a shoe off the horse's foot or loosen shoes. This means the farrier will have to come out to replace them which will increase costs. It can also pose a danger if a shoe is left in the field somewhere. A horse could roll or tread on it and injure themselves, particularly if there are nails left in the shoe.

Figure 36: Bricks and gravel have been laid here to help prevent muddy areas.

If gateways do become muddy they can be managed by removing about six inches of top soil, spreading a layer of broken bricks over the problematic area then adding a layer of gravel on top of that **(Fig. 36)**. This allows the water to drain away without the ground getting churned up. This can also be useful in other mud prone areas such as by water buckets or water troughs.

Gateways should be kept clear of any obstacles and overhanging trees or bushes. This is to make it easy and safe to get horses in and out of the field. Horses are quite often excited when being turned out or brought in if they know they are coming in to be fed so it is best if there is nothing in the way for both the horse and the handler to trip over or get caught on.

Shelter

The purpose of the field shelter is to protect the horse from harsh weather such as wind, rain and sun, making them more comfortable when turned out. Leaving a horse in a field with no form of shelter could prove to be fatal. If the horse

Figure 37: This donkey is using the fence to shelter from the sun but if it were to rain the donkey would be very exposed.

cannot find any shade on a hot day they could die from heat

57

exhaustion so it is an important feature to make available in each field.

There should be enough shelter for the number of horses in the field. Man-made field shelters are on average about half the size of a stable. It should be enough space for one to two horses to shelter under and it should ideally have two openings or one large opening. This is so that both horses can easily get in and out without getting in each other's way which helps to reduce the risk of fighting and injury. Tall walls and hedging can also provide a level of shelter though these are less beneficial when it is raining **(Fig. 37)**.

Grass Management

A suitable field should have good quality ground with a good covering of grass. The grass should be good quality but should not be too rich as this can cause laminitis. The grass will start to grow at around March to April and will stop growing when the ground starts to get frosty near winter. It is then that you will need to start supplementing field kept horses with hay.

To promote good overall growth and to help get rid of tall plants and weeds the field should be topped. Tractors can sometimes be seen doing this in larger fields. They tow or push around machinery, from behind or to the side, which cuts the grass. This makes the field look tidier and the horse is more likely to graze a larger percentage of pasture if there is not an abundance of weeds present.

Figure 38: This field has been sectioned off to allow the grass to grow. This can be seen by the difference in grass colour.

To ensure there is always a good supply of grass available you can section off part of a field for the horses to go in and graze while another section (the same size) is left empty for the grass to grow **(Fig. 38)**. Once the horses have exhausted their section of grass and it is too short for any more grazing they can then be moved onto the section where the grass has had chance to grow. Once this section has been grazed down the previous section should have grown back and the horses can go back in there. Make sure droppings are always removed before leaving the grass to grow back to help reduce the spread of worm eggs.

If a horse is likely to become laminitic from having access to too much grass all at once try putting them in a field that has been grazed well with a section of well grown grass next to it. Using electric tape fencing and some stakes you can move the fence along a bit every day or so to reveal a fresh strip of grass for the horse. The opposite side should be moved along too in the same direction so the horse has the same amount of field available to them all the time and this allows the grazed area to grow back. If the grass is quite rich then it might be worth limiting the amount of time the horses spend in the field. If you want to keep them turned out longer then allowing them a strip of well grown grass each day while keeping them in a well grazed field will help to avoid them taking in too much rich grass.

Always check the field is clear of rubbish, holes and unnecessary objects. This will help keep the field in tip top condition and it will be safer for the horses too. If there is a problem and the field is unsafe stop using the field until the problem is rectified. Risking it and putting the horses in there anyway could lead to a hefty vet bill!

Dangerous Plants

Spotting and Removing

There are a number of plants that are poisonous to horses. Some will make the horse ill and others are deadly. The fields should be checked for these plants approximately once a week as some plants can sprout up quickly without being noticed. To get a good look at the fields you should walk the perimeter of each field then zig zag from one end to the other. If the field is particularly large you should try to vary where you walk each time you check in case you missed something on your last field check.

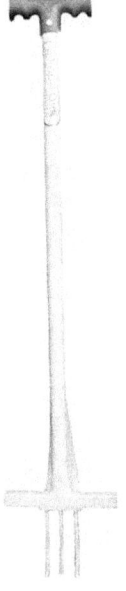

Figure 39: A ragwort fork. The prongs help to pull the plant up by the roots.

If poisonous plants are present they should either be removed by the roots or fenced off. If removing by the roots you must try to make sure you remove the entire root else there is a chance the plant will grow back. There is a special tool **(Fig. 39)** for doing this which makes the job a lot easier and also saves you having to bend over too much which is always a bonus! Digging up weeds when the ground is soft will also make it easier. Pulling up plants on a hot day with hard soil will just cause the plant to break off at the base and digging up the plant to remove the roots will just be hard work. Gloves should always be worn when handling poisonous plants. This is to protect yourself from the toxins and it stops you transferring any harmful material onto anything the horse may come into contact with too. Once out of the ground, the plants should be placed straight into a plastic bag to avoid the spread of seeds then burned or sent to a specialist registered company that disposes of poisonous and controlled plants.

Another way to remove unwanted plants is to spray them with weed killer. If you are doing this you should remove the horses from that field for a few weeks and make sure the plants have gone before allowing the horses back into that field. Plants that cannot be removed, such as trees or hedges, should be fenced off – not just around the base of the plant but as far as the tree or hedge overhangs. This is because if the horse can still reach the plant or if it drops its leaves, fruit or nuts onto the ground where the horse can reach then the horse is still at risk of being poisoned.

The following are all poisonous to horses:

Toxic Plants

Ragwort – This starts off as a leafy plant that is flat on the ground and resembles a rosette **(Fig. 40)**. It then grows into a tall plant (up to 150cm) and produces yellow flowers from June to October. Ragwort is highly toxic, both fresh or dead, and the whole plant above ground level is poisonous. If a horse has been eating ragwort he will go off his food which will lead to weight loss and even anorexia. The lack of nutrition from not eating will cause the horse's coat to look dull and poor and he will be ill thrift as he fails to thrive. He may experience convulsions, lack of co-ordination and have changes in his temperature, pulse and respiration. The normal behaviour of the horse will change as their condition changes and deteriorates. The horse will start to look jaundice which will be due to liver damage which can lead to liver failure and then death.

Figure 40: The rosette of a ragwort plant before it grows tall and flowers.

Buttercups – These are quite common in fields and can grow quite tall. They have a bright, cup shaped, yellow flower **(Fig. 41)**. The stems and fresh leaves are poisonous and if eaten the horse may experience oral irritation, salivation, colic-like symptoms due to abdominal pain and diarrhoea (possibly bloody). The reaction will be self-limiting as the horse will lose its appetite and stop eating the problem plant and will therefore start to get better. In general, horses tend to avoid eating buttercups if there is plenty of better forage readily

Figure 41: Tall buttercups like these are more commonly found in fields.

available but if this does become a problem then the buttercups should be sprayed with weed killer and the field rested or you can top the field to remove them straight away though this will not stop them growing back.

Privet – This plant makes for great hedging but it is poisonous so if it is used it should also be fenced off to prevent the horses getting to it. It has creamy coloured flowers **(Fig. 42)** and the whole plant is poisonous – the berries even more so. This plant can cause death by poisoning in as little as four hours so ideally its use should be avoided completely. Symptoms of poisoning can include staggering, uncoordinated movements, paralysis, dilated

Figure 42: The leaves and creamy-white flowers of privet.

pupils, a compromised gastrointestinal tract, diarrhoea and convulsions.

Yew – This is an ornamental evergreen tree with small, dark green, spiky leaves. It produces bright red berries which are about the size of a grape and they have a small hole in one end **(Fig. 43)**. This tree is extremely toxic (both fresh and dry) as just one mouthful can kill a horse in just five minutes. The toxin causes the cardiac and / or respiratory system to

Figure 43: The red berries and spiky leaves of a yew tree.

collapse. If symptoms are shown then they will present themselves as a slow heart rate, trembling, breathlessness, colic-like symptoms and diarrhoea. First aid is rarely effective as the horse will die before anything can be done though if veterinary treatment is sought quickly enough then there may be a very small chance the horse could survive. This tree should be kept out of the yard and fields as it is so dangerous. If there is one present then it should be fenced off and be careful to clear away any cuttings as these are just as dangerous. The berries themselves are not dangerous but it is inadvisable to allow the horse to eat them.

Oak – This can become quite a large tree and both the leaves and acorns **(Fig. 44)** are poisonous. The taste can be quite attractive to horses and once they have tasted the leaves and acorns they may begin to actively seek out more. A small amount may not be too harmful but if the horse has access to this tree then they are likely to continue poisoning themselves. Symptoms may include abdominal pain, bloody

Figure 44: The acorns and leaves of an oak tree.

urine, constipation followed by bloody diarrhoea, lack of appetite, a starring coat and a depressed mood. Poisoning usually happens from spring to autumn when the leaves are green and the acorns are present. Ideally, this tree should be fenced off with no overhanging branches to prevent acorns dropping into the field. If other food sources are plentiful such as grass and hay this should help to prevent the horse trying to reach a nearby oak tree.

Ivy – This can be an attractive plant if grown in a controlled manner up walls or fencing but care should be taken as to where it is allowed to creep to **(Fig. 45)**. It can spread very quickly, not just up walls and fencing but along the ground and around trees or anything that comes into its path. This is why if it is being grown for ornamental

Figure 45: Ivy creeping along a wall.

reasons it should be kept on top of so it does not go wild and spread to areas that the horses can reach. This plant grows in the form of long vines. The leaves are dark green and the berries are black. Trimming the vines back will help to prevent the spread of this plant but it can be difficult to get rid of it altogether and it will grow back quite quickly. Both leaves and berries are poisonous but the toxicity is low. Signs of poisoning are irritation of the mouth, stomach irritation (may show colic-like symptoms), diarrhoea and difficulty breathing. If the horse has consumed a large quantity of ivy then coma and even death could follow.

Laburnum – This is a large tree that produces yellow flowers that hang down in the form of pedecels **(Fig. 46)**. It is an ornamental tree and while it would look beautiful in the middle of your field every part of it is poisonous to horses, especially the bark and the seeds. Symptoms of poisoning from this tree are salivation, colic-like symptoms, diarrhoea,

Figure 46: Long golden chains of blossom from a laburnum tree.

uncoordinated movements, convulsions, dilated pupils and even death if consumed in large quantities. You could still have this beautiful tree in the middle of your field...but it should have fencing all around it!

Foxglove – This plant grows in the form of a long stem that produces tubular shaped flowers that vary in colour **(Fig. 47)**. They can be purple, pink, white or yellow and are very pretty but the whole plant, including the roots and seeds, is poisonous. The leaves on the upper part of the stem are the most toxic and these could potentially cause death. Horses would not usually graze on these plants but they may be ingested if they found their way into the horse's hay as they are still toxic once they are dried out. Signs of poisoning are irregular heartbeat or heart failure (caused by cardiac glycosides found

Figure 47: The leafy foxglove with bell-shaped flowers.

in foxglove), drowsiness (caused by bradycardia – slow heartbeat), abdominal pain (may show colic-like symptoms), diarrhoea and convulsions. Even though horses may not choose to graze on foxglove it should still be pulled up by the roots to remove the risk of a potential poisoning.

Deadly nightshade – This is a branched shrub that produces large ovate leaves, purple bell-shaped flowers and black berries (**Fig. 48, 49**). It is rarely eaten by horses if there are plenty of other food sources to graze on such as grass and hay but if it were to find its way into the horse's hay then poisoning can occur. Signs of poisoning could be instability (caused by loss of muscle control), disorientation, dilated pupils and colic-like symptoms. Death can also occur so seek veterinary treatment as soon as possible.

If you suspect that a horse has been poisoned or has eaten a poisonous plant then contact the vet straight away, even if the horse is not showing signs of poisoning. It is better to be safe than sorry and the sooner the vet can diagnose and treat the horse the better as this could improve the horse's chance of survival.

Figure 48: The flowers of deadly nightshade.

Figure 49: The black berries and leaves of deadly nightshade.

Feeding

Feed Types

There is a large variety of feeds available for horses to the point where it can be overwhelming picking the right feed for your horse. Most of these feeds contain ingredients from the list below but in different quantities and varieties according to what type of diet they are catering for. These raw ingredients are called straights and they can be bought either just as they are or in the form of a cube or mix where the ingredients have been put together for you to help form a balanced diet for your horse.

Ingredient	Feed Type	Nutritional Benefit
Flaked maize – Sweetcorn that has been cooked and flaked.	Concentrates	Fed mainly to horses in slow work. It is fattening, gives energy and is easily digested.
Crushed barley – A small grain, golden in colour. Once crushed or rolled it will start to decline in nutritional value.	Concentrates	High in starch energy. Does not make horse as hyper as oats might. Good for weight gain.
Cooked barley – Grains of barley that have been boiled as they are.	Concentrates	Digestible energy is raised by 3% when the grains of barley are cooked.
Rolled oats – The husk of the oat is broken by rolling the grains. This allows the horse access to the nutrients.	Concentrates	Has a lower digestible energy percentage than maize and barley.

Naked oats – A grain that is grown to have a loose husk that is shed when harvested. This makes it easier to digest.	Concentrates	They have 1/3 more digestible energy and protein than a standard oat. They are also high in oil. Provide less fibre due to lack of husk.
Peas – This vegetable is soaked or crushed to be made palatable.	Concentrates	Provides a similar amount of digestible energy as barley. They are low in fat and are a good source of protein.
Beans – Green beans are a common choice of beans to feed.	Concentrates	A good source of energy, protein, vitamins and minerals.
Sugar beet – A root vegetable in pellet form that is soaked to make it safe for horses to eat.	Succulents	Provides a similar amount of energy as oats but comes from digestible fibre rather than starch.
Carrots – This long orange vegetable should be cut into fingers to encourage chewing and prevent choking.	Concentrates / Succulents	They provide a high level of carotene and are full of water, vitamins and minerals.
Apples – A round green or red fruit that should be cut into fingers to encourage chewing and prevent choking.	Succulents	They provide water, vitamins and minerals. They are a tasty addition to feeds or a healthy treat.

Haylage – Hay that has been wrapped in polythene and left to ferment for around 10 weeks.	Succulents / Roughage	Contains more moisture and sugar than normal hay and provides more energy so is given to horses with a bigger work load.
Grass – Fresh green stalks that are grazed by the horse when turned out.	Roughage	Grass is succulent and is a very good source of fibre.
Hay – Long grass that is cut and dried. Various grasses can be used.	Roughage	Hay is a good source of fibre. It also provides protein, calcium and carotene.
Chaff – Chopped up stalks that are sometimes coated in molasses. It is added to feed to encourage the horse to chew.	Roughage	Chaff offers fibre and bulk to a feed and if molassed it can offer a small amount of energy.
Alfalfa – Also known as Lucerne. It is a plant from the pea family which produces purple flowers.	Roughage	Contains highly digestible fibre and is high in protein. Lower levels of sugar and carbohydrates compared to normal hay.

Rules of Feeding

There are a number of rules that should be followed when feeding a horse. These help to makes sure that the horse receives an adequate diet for the work they do and environment they live in.

- ⋏ Feed little and often

    - ⋏ Horses are trickle feeders because their stomachs are only small. Too much food can cause blockages in their intestines which can bring on a bout of colic.

- ⋏ Wash feed utensils after every use

    - ⋏ This prevents bacteria building up on the utensils. It also makes sure that any drugs that are put in the feeds are only ingested by the horse that was prescribed it.

- ⋏ Include a moist, succulent food in the horse's feed daily

    - ⋏ The horse's digestive system works best when being provided with a regular supply of grass which is moist and succulent so this should be replicated at feed times.

- ⋏ Feeds should cater for work load and appetite

    - ⋏ Horses need the correct energy levels for them to cope with the work they are doing and to keep the right amount of weight on them.

- ⋏ Feed plenty of forage

    - ⋏ The horse's digestive system is designed to always have grass and other roughage passing through it like it would in the wild.

⅄ Never work a horse until at least an hour after being fed

> ⅄ The horse's stomach sits close to the lungs which need to expand when being exercised so the stomach will need time to partially empty to allow room for this to happen. Also, the horse's blood supply needs to be focused on the stomach and intestines for the food to be digested rather than flowing around the body to help cool the horse down during exercise.

⅄ Water should always be made available

> ⅄ A horse can quickly become dehydrated and will not survive without water. A lack of it will cause the horse's condition to quickly deteriorate. Water also helps move food through the digestive system and so helps to prevent colic.

⅄ An established diet should be changed gradually over a period of time

> ⅄ The horse's gut flora needs time to adapt to changes in the diet or else new food may not get digested properly. Diarrhoea can be a result of this.

⅄ Keep to a feeding routine

> ⅄ Horses like routine and changing something important to them such as a feed routine could upset them.

⅄ Always feed good quality food

> ⅄ A good quality feed will offer more nutrients and is less likely to make the horse ill.

Feed Quantities

The quantity of feed given will vary from horse to horse. This is because each horse is different and may have different requirements. The amount of food a horse needs to eat will depend on the following:

1. The overall size and weight of the horse – the horse needs to eat the equivalent of 2.5% of its bodyweight daily

2. Appetite

3. Work load

4. Age

5. Medical conditions

6. How good the handler or rider is. This is because if a horse is fed lots of food that is going to pump him full of energy and has a beginner rider plonked on his back there is going to be an accident!

These are the main points that should be considered when choosing what to feed and working out how much should be fed. We now have all of the information we need to work out how much to feed our horse. So how do we put all of this information together to get the right amount of feed? There are a couple of ways to work this out.

Method 1

Using a weigh bridge or weigh tape work out the weight of the horse. If, for example, the horse weighs 500kg we would need to find 2.5% of 500kg which we can do by using the following calculation:

$500 \div 100 \times 2.5 = 12.5$

So this horse will need to be fed 12.5kg of food every day. This will include hard feed and roughage (including grass though this is obviously difficult to measure).

Method 2

This method, simple as it is, is more of an approximation and is used if you do not know the weight of the horse. Take the height of the horse (in hands) and minus 3. This will give you the weight of food in kg that should be fed. So for a 15hh horse:

$$15 - 3 = 12$$

This horse will need to be fed approximately 12kg of food every day. If you prefer to work in pounds rather than kilograms then you can take the horse's height, double it then minus 2 and this will give you the weight of food in pounds that the horse should be given every day. This method is less accurate as it does not take into account the overall size of the horse. You could have a lightweight 16hh Thoroughbred horse and you could have a heavyweight 16hh Shire – the Shire would obviously need more feed per day as its body weight will be greater than that of the Thoroughbred which is why method 1 is more accurate.

Once you have figured out how much feed your horse needs you then have to divide this between concentrates and forage. To do this you need to take into account how much work the horse does and what his temperament is like.

Work Load	Feed Ratio
Light Work – gentle daily hacking. Maybe a show at the weekends with a little bit of canter.	15% to 20% Concentrates – 85% to 80% Roughage
Medium Work – Hacking and schooling with some jumping almost daily while showing most weekends.	25% Concentrates – 75% Roughage
Hard Work – Competition training almost daily. Jumping, cross country, galloping, regular shows and events.	30% to 35% Concentrates – 70% to 65% Roughage

The horse needs at least 65% of its diet to be roughage so a hard working horse should not be given less than this.

So if we want to work out the quantity of concentrate and roughage to give to our light working 15hh horse that needs 12kg of feed we can do the following:

$$\frac{\text{Total weight of feed}}{100} \times \text{Percentage of concentrates} = 12 \div 100 \times 15 = 1.8$$

So we are going to feed this horse 1.8kg of concentrates per day.

$$\frac{\text{Total weight of feed}}{100} \times \text{Percentage of roughage} = 12 \div 100 \times 85 = 10.2$$

And we are going to feed this horse 10.2kg of roughage per day (this includes grass).

Treatment Feeds

There are a couple of
different reasons why you
may need to give a horse a
treatment feed. They could
be ill, underweight or have
few or no teeth. A
common example of one
of these feeds is a bran

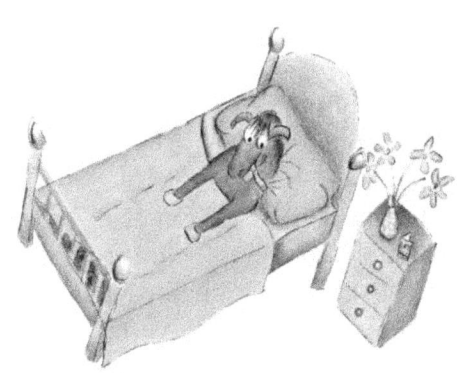

mash. This encourages the horse to eat because it is palatable and
easy to digest. Once made up, the mash is tempting due to its
pleasant aroma which will help to encourage a sick horse to eat. It
will also help them pass droppings if this is an issue. It is easy for
older horses to eat because of its soft, mushy consistency. Even
though this mash is helpful for the reasons mentioned above, it
should not be fed in large quantities as the bran will cause an
imbalance in the horse's calcium : phosphorous levels.

How to make a bran mash:

1. Put 2 – 4 cups of bran into a clean bucket (this will vary
   with the size of the horse)

2. Pour boiling water over the bran until it is wet

3. Stir well

4. Cover and leave until it is warm – it should be crumbly
   and moist

5. Add a small amount of molasses to improve flavour

6. Add succulents such as carrot and apple to add flavour,
   vitamins and nutrients

7. Add medication to the feed if it has been prescribed and
   stir it in well

8. Feed while still warm

Great care should be taken when using medication in feeds. Be absolutely certain that the right medication is put in the right feed in the right quantity. Mixing it in well will help to prevent the horse noticing it and eating around it. Bowls and utensils should be thoroughly washed after every use when they have come into contact with medication. This is because if a horse consumes a medicine that is not meant for them it could make them ill. If the horse does become ill and you are unaware that they have consumed a medicine that has not been prescribed to them it could be harder for the vet to diagnose the problem making it harder to treat. Another reason why it is important to avoid contaminating another horse's feed with traces of medication is because if that horse is used for showing they may have to be drugs tested. If their test shows up positive for certain drugs the rider and possibly the horse will be disqualified from that event and the rider could be suspended for 2 years. There will be a fine on top of this and there may even be legal costs. People who support the rider may also be affected by a positive test too. People such as vets, grooms and trainers could all be suspended as will be the horse involved. It is not worth being sloppy when handling medicine as so many people could be affected by the consequences so it is better to be careful and get into a good hygienic routine with cleaning utensils and bowls and throwing away any empty medicine containers.

Worming

It is important to worm a horse regularly because they can ingest worm eggs while grazing. The eggs themselves come from a small number of worms that already live inside

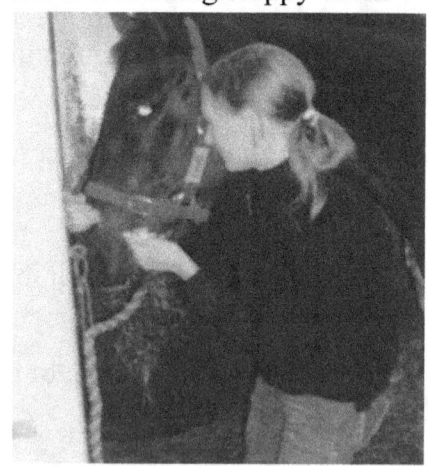

Figure 50: Administering a wormer through a syringe. Notice how the handler's right hand is over the horse's nose to prevent them throwing their head up.

76

the horse and the eggs that are produced are released from the body in the horse's droppings. This is why it is so important to pick up droppings from the field on a daily basis. Even though the horse already has a small number of worms in their system you need to try to prevent the horse from becoming infested with worms as this will begin to affect the horse's health. A regular worming regime and careful field management will all help to keep the number of worms in the horse's system to a minimum. A sample of the horse's droppings can also be given to the vet for a worm egg count. This gives the vet an idea of how many worms are in the horse's system and if any action needs to be taken.

Worming medication can be given to the horse either in liquid form via a syringe **(Fig. 50, 51)** or in tablet form which can be mixed into the horse's feed. Some tablets have a pleasant flavour to help prevent the horse avoiding the medication.

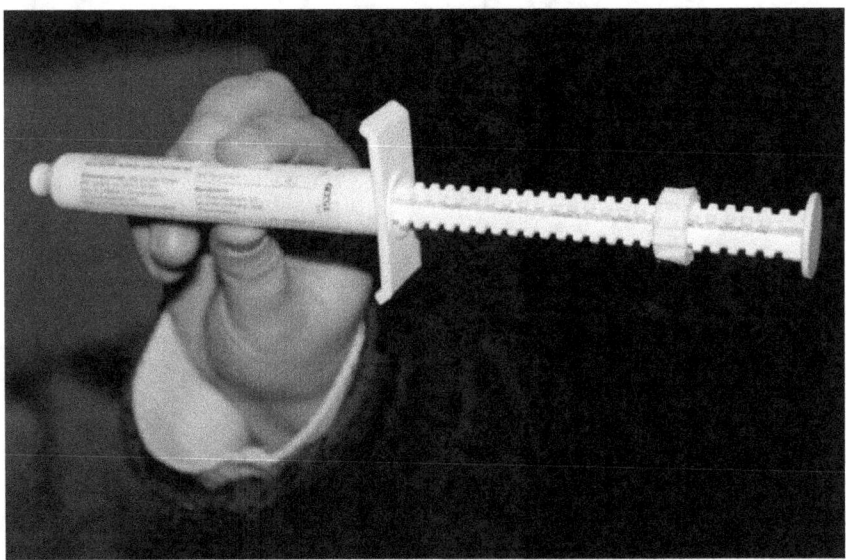

Figure 51: A worming syringe allows you to squirt the correct dose of medication into the horse's mouth.

Showing

Not all yards will be involved with showing their horses but there are some that take a few of their horses to shows regularly and even compete with them for a living.

There are shows for a variety of disciplines such as the following:

- ⅄ Dressage

- ⅄ Show jumping

- ⅄ Cross country

- ⅄ Eventing

- ⅄ Driving

- ⅄ In-hand showing

- ⅄ Racing

Usually, it is the job of the groom to prepare the horses before they are transported to the show. They then get the horses ready at the show and help warm them up and cool them down. Once the horses have finished the groom should make them comfortable then prepare them for travelling back to the yard when it is time to go. In addition to tending to the horses the groom may also have to look after any paperwork and keep track of which horses need to be where at what times. This will help keep the people showing the horses organised and in the right place at the right time.

Tack

There are many different types of tack. What is used depends on what the horse is used for, what level they are working at and the level of the handler. These variations of saddles and bridles are all based on a basic saddle and bridle. Be aware that different countries also have different tack so the English saddle and bridle, for example, is very different to the American saddle and bridle. The basic English saddle which has been designed to be used for most activities is called the general purpose saddle and the basic English bridle is called the snaffle bridle.

The General Purpose Saddle

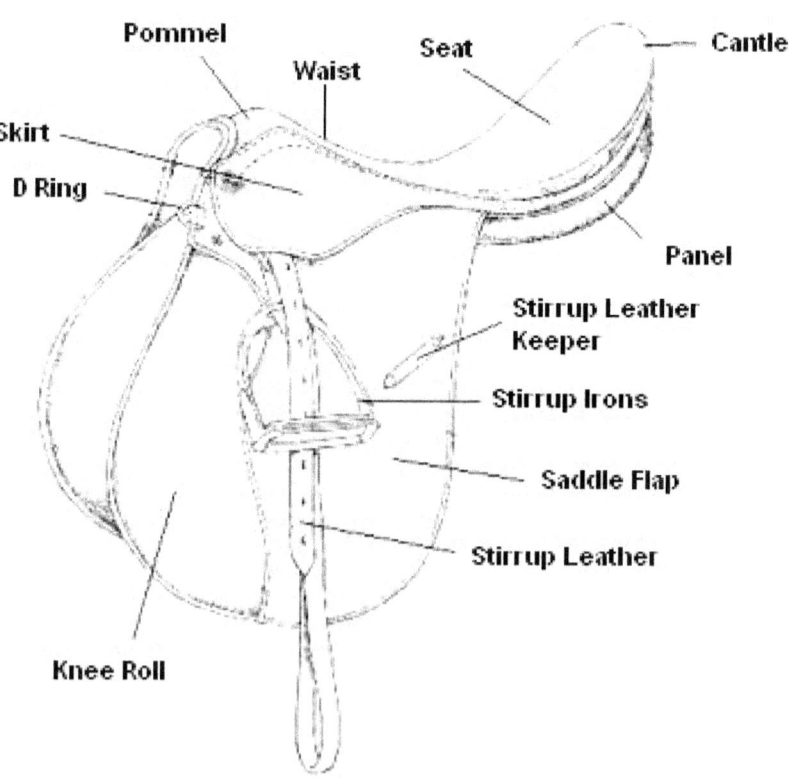

Underneath The Saddle Flap

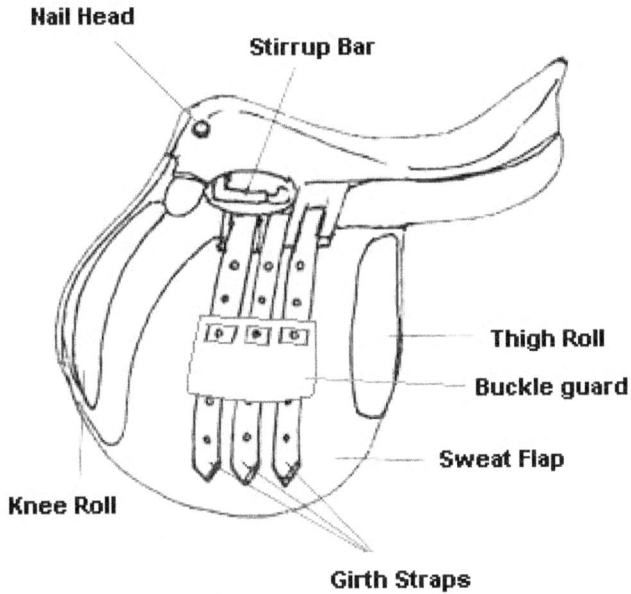

Saddle Tree

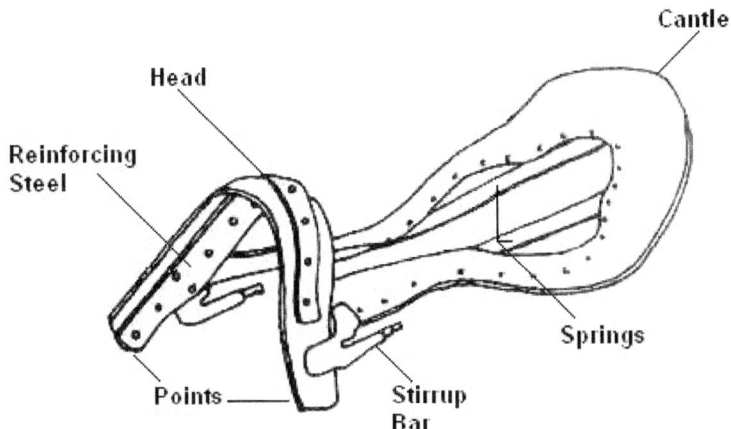

Under The Saddle

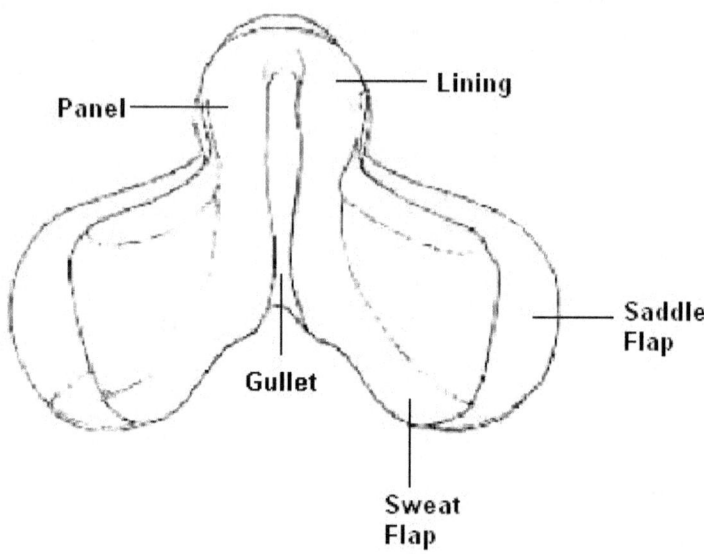

The Snaffle Bridle

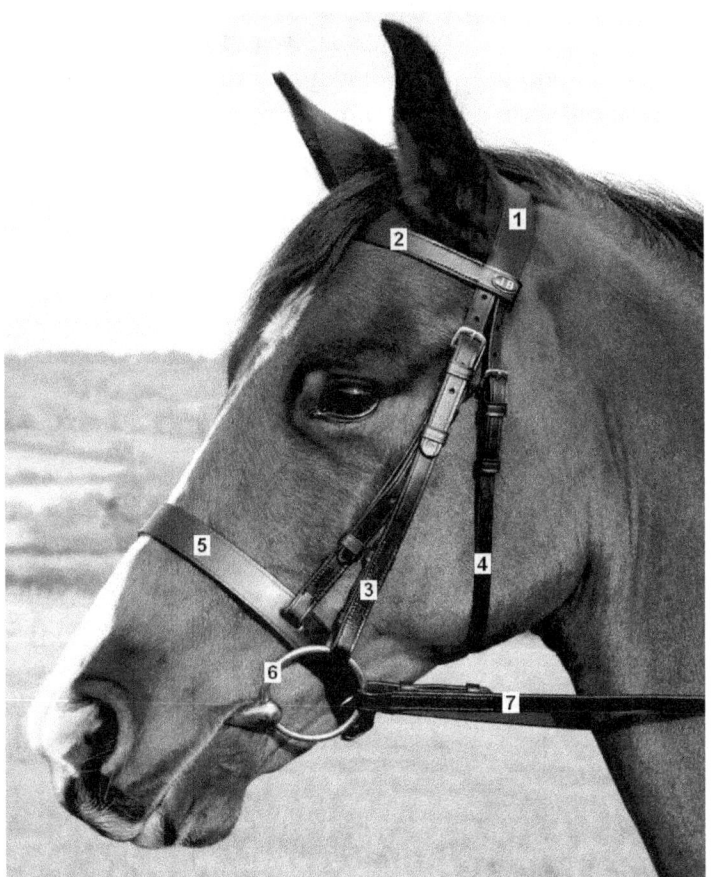

Key

1. Head Piece
2. Brow Band
3. Cheek Piece
4. Throat Lash
5. Nose Band
6. Bit
7. Reins

Tacking up

Tacking up may seem complicated to begin with and not all horses are tacked up in the same way because they may have different tack but with a bit of experience it soon becomes second nature.

To apply a snaffle bridle and general purpose saddle follow the directions below:

1. Bring the tack and a grooming kit to the area where you are going to tack up.

2. Tie the horse up using a head collar and lead rope.

3. Remove any rugs and give the horse a quick groom to remove any dirt and bedding. Pick the horse's feet out too.

4. Place the saddle gently onto the horse's back just over the withers. It can then be pulled back slightly so it sits comfortably into the shape of the horse and so all of the hair underneath is lying flat.

5. Pull the numnah or saddle pad up at the withers so it follows the shape of the pommel. This prevents it putting pressure on the withers.

6. Bring the girth underneath the horse and fasten it to the girth straps on the left side of the saddle. It should be sitting just behind the horse's elbows. Tighten the girth gradually to avoid pinching the horse. You should be able to fit two fingers between the girth and the horse.

7. If the stirrups are dangling down, run the stirrup iron up the stirrup leather closest to the saddle then put the stirrup leather through the iron towards the saddle and pull it down to secure the iron. Do this to both stirrups **(Fig. 52)**.

8. Take the bridle and make sure the noseband and throat lash are both undone.

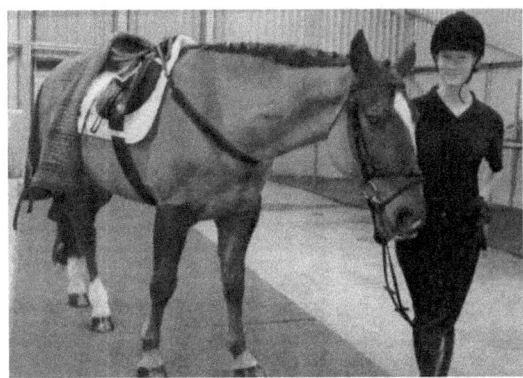

9. Remove the head collar and put the reins over the horse's head onto their neck then slide the bridle up the horse's head and put the bit in the horse's mouth. If the horse refuses to open their mouth slide your thumb into the side of their mouth to the part where there are no teeth – this usually encourages them to open up!

Figure 52: This horse has just been tacked up. Notice the position of the saddle on his back. The saddle is being prevented from slipping back by a breast collar (positioned just below his neck). Notice also how the stirrups have been run up. This prevents them catching on anything while he is not being ridden. There is a rug over his hind quarters to help keep him warm since he has been clipped.

10. Slide the head piece over both ears and gently pull any forelock through so it sits on top of the brow band.

11. Fasten the noseband so it sits underneath the cheek pieces. You should be able to fit one finger between the noseband and the horse.

12. Fasten the throat lash. You should be able to fit four fingers between the throat lash and the horse.

13. Finally, make sure all straps on both the saddle and bridle are tucked into their keepers.

14. If the horse is going to be left for a while twist the reins a couple of times under the horse's head and thread the throat lash through them and do it up. This prevents them coming back over the horse's head if they put their head down. Put the head collar back on over the bridle so the horse is now tied up again. Now is a good time to put on any boots or polo wraps if they are needed.

To remove tack:

1. Put a head collar and lead rope on the horse and tie them up with a quick release knot.

2. Gently undo the girth (the stirrups should have been run up after dismounting) then pull the saddle off to the left side of the horse by taking the pommel in your left hand and the cantle in your right hand. Put the saddle somewhere out of the way or over the stable door.

3. Remove any boots or polo wraps and put them out of the way.

4. Remove the head collar and take a hold of the reins immediately to remove the bridle. It is at this point a horse may walk off to have a roll which can be dangerous if any tack is still on and the tack can get damaged too!

5. Undo the noseband and throat lash.

6. Take the reins over the horse's head then pull the bridle off down the horse's head from the head piece, allowing the horse time to let go of the bit. Place the bridle out of the horse's reach and off the floor somewhere. Over the stable door is fine.

7. Sponge off any sweaty areas and rug the horse up if one is being used.

8. Clean the tack then put it away.

Tack Cleaning

Cleaning tack is important as this keeps it in good condition. Tack is expensive to buy so looking after it properly will make it last longer. Giving it a quick clean down after each use is a good habit to get into and will prevent long, grubby tack cleaning sessions. It will also be more comfortable for your horse as sticky, dirty tack can rub and lead to sores.

There is a variety of products available to help keep your tack in tip top condition and you could spend a lot of money thinking you could preserve your tack longer if you buy more products. This is not the case! All you really need is a bucket of water, a sponge, saddle soap, a brush and proper storage. If you keep the tack clean and conditioned and store it off the floor in a dry, well ventilated place this will keep it in good condition.

So How's It Done?

Tack cleaning is a simple and easy process which can become hard, dirty work if not done regularly. Follow these simple steps after each ride and you will make light work of it!

1. Collect your things. You will need a bucket of clean, warm water (cold is fine but less pleasant for you!), a clean sponge, saddle soap, a brush and your tack.

2. Brush any sand out of the stirrup irons using a bristly brush or wire brush.

3. Rinse the bit off in the bucket of water.

4. Wet the sponge and wipe away any dirt, sweat, sand and hair from the saddle, bridle and girth. Concentrate more on the areas that come into contact with the horse.

5. Rinse and squeeze the sponge out so it is only damp then apply a small amount of saddle soap to the sponge. Wipe this over the saddle and bridle, avoiding any parts that are not leather. If it froths up then your sponge is too wet. Do not rinse off when finished.

6. Put the tack away in a clean, dry, well ventilated environment and keep it away from the floor.

Despite it's name, saddle soap is not actually used to clean tack. When you apply it as described above this adds moisture to the leather, leaving it soft and supple and in good condition. It helps to prevent drying out which leads to cracking and flaking of the leather which can happen when tack is left or not looked after properly.

Preparing The Horse

Making the horse look clean, tidy and well-presented can be a big job and can take some practice. The mane and tail need to be prepared according to the show they are going to and they may need to be clipped or trimmed in places to neaten them up.

Different shows require different 'hair styles' for horses so make sure you are doing the right one before you start. Ask if you are not sure!

Typically, a horse's mane will be put into several plaits which are then rolled up into balls along the crest of the horse. This is usually done for most equine sports. The tail may also be plaited. This is slightly trickier than the mane but if you have a friend you can practice on this can help a lot!

Grooming Kit

In order to get the horse looking spick and span you will need a grooming kit and a bucket of water. In your grooming kit you will need:

- ⅄ Rubber curry comb

- ⅄ Plastic curry comb

⅄ Metal curry comb

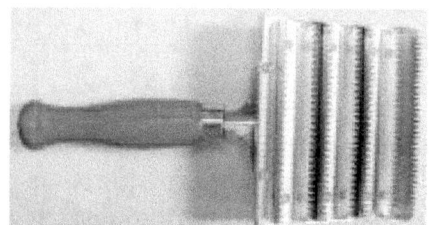

⅄ Mane comb

⅄ Pulling comb

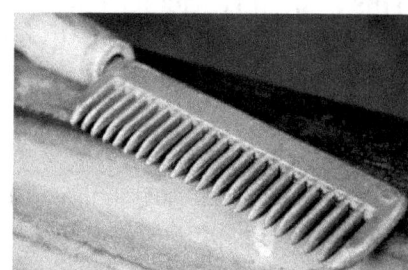

⅄ Two clean sponges

⅄ Hoof pick

- ⋏ Small rubber bands

- ⋏ Tail bandage

- ⋏ Dandy brush

- ⋏ Body brush

- ⋏ Water brush

✠ Sweat scraper

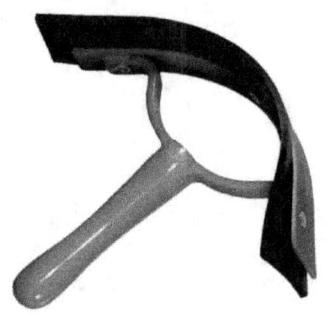

✠ Stable rubber

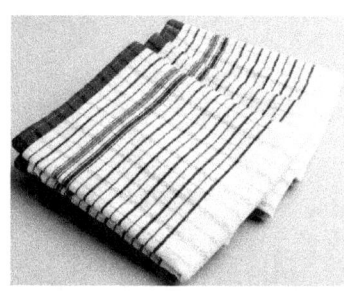

✠ Cactus Cloth

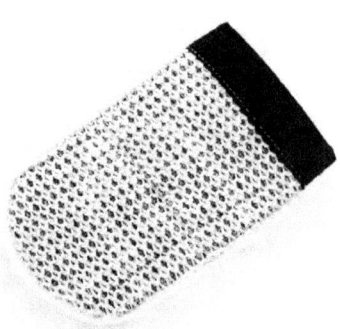

✠ Hoof oil

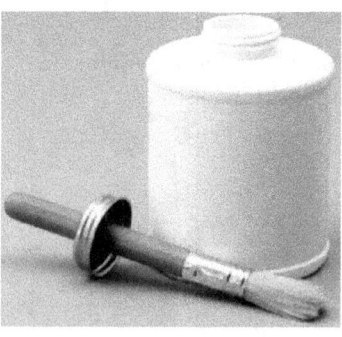

Grooming

To prepare a horse for showing you will need to give them a very
thorough groom. If they are particularly dirty with mud or stains
then it may be best to give them a bath first. Grooming thoroughly
and plaiting can take a little while but once you have got it
mastered you can have a horse prepared in around 1 – 2 hours.

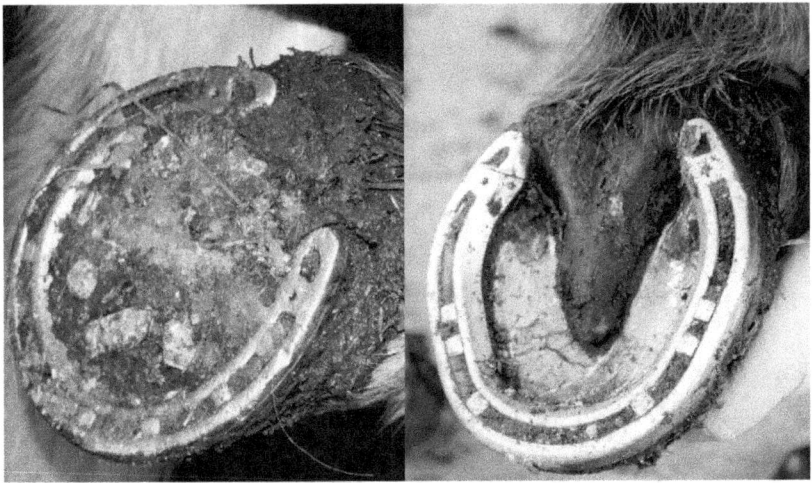

*Figure 53: Scrape the hoof pick down the grooves either side of the
frog (triangular bit) toward the toe (bottom of picture).*

1. Collect your grooming kit, bucket of warm water, skip,
    shovel and broom and take them to where you intend to
    groom the horse. Keep your tools and kit out of the horse's
    reach but somewhere accessible to you.

2. Lead the horse to where you intend to groom them and
    secure them using a quick release knot.

3. Start by picking out the horse's feet. This is done by
    scraping the hoof pick downwards from the heel to the toe
    and around the shoes. Be careful around the frog as this is
    sensitive **(Fig. 53)**. This is also a good time to check the
    shoes are still on firmly.

4. Sweep away anything you picked out of the horse's feet. If at any time the horse passes droppings, shovel it up and put it in the skip. Sweep again to prevent the horse's feet getting dirty.

5. Brush the horse's mane and forelock with the mane comb.

6. Undo the quick release knot but leave the rope through the breakable string. Undo the noseband of the head collar and move the head collar down the horse's neck a couple of inches

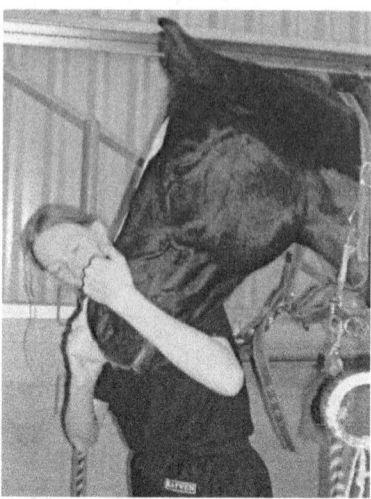

Figure 54: Hold the horse's head like this when grooming, sponging or washing the face. Notice what has been done to the head collar.

(Fig. 54). Gently brush the horse's face with the soft body brush, holding the horse's head with one arm under the neck and over the nose from the other side. This holds them steady and prevents them throwing their head up.

7. Take a clean sponge and dampen it in the bucket of warm water. Gently sponge the horse's eyes from the corner outwards **(Fig. 55)**. Make sure you thoroughly rinse the sponge out between cleaning each eye. Hold the horse's head as described in step 6 **(Fig. 54)** while doing this.

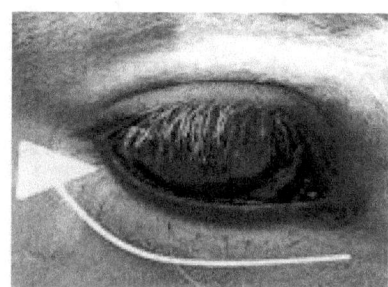

Figure 55: Wipe from the inside corner out.

8. Rinse the sponge again then gently clean around the nostrils and lips **(Fig. 54)**. Hold the horse's head as described in step 6 while doing this. Once you have finished this move the head collar back up the horse's neck to its normal position, fasten the noseband and tie the lead rope back into a quick release knot.

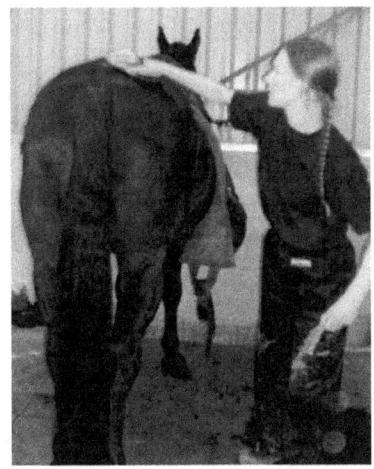

9. Brush the horse's whole body and legs **(Fig. 56)** in a circular motion with the rubber curry comb. This will bring to the surface any mud, dirt, scurf and loose hair. (Gently use a plastic curry comb on any areas caked with mud).

Figure 56: Grooming the horse while leaving him rugged up (quartering). Notice how the rug has been folded back and the surcingles have been tied together to prevent them hanging down too far.

10. If there are lots of loose hairs and scurf quickly brush it away with the dandy brush (do not use this on the face or clipped areas of the horse as the bristles are too harsh).

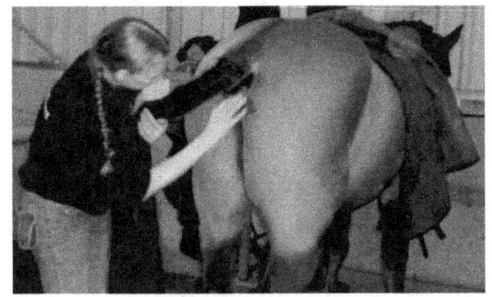

Figure 57: Notice how the person is standing to the side while working behind the horse. The rug has also been folded back so it is well out of the way.

11. Use the soft body brush to remove any remaining scurf and hair. Starting from the top of the horse's neck work your way down to the withers, back, rump and down the body to the legs

then feet. Scrape the body brush off with the metal curry comb in between every few strokes of brushing. Tap the metal curry comb on the floor every few minutes to gather a pile of dirt and hair which can be picked up when you have finished brushing.

12. If there are any stains on the horse that are still present after all that brushing give it a rub with a cactus cloth then remove any loose hair or dirt with the body brush. If this does not work try sponging it off with warm water.

13. Take a different sponge then clean around the horse's dock and bottom **(Fig. 57)**.

14. Brush the very top of the horse's tail with the body brush then run your fingers through the rest of the tail to remove any knots. Do this with a small section of hair at a time.

15. Dampen the water brush and brush this over the top of the tail. If the mane does not need plaiting then give it a quick brush over with a dampened water brush too. This gives the hair a neat finish.

16. Apply the tail bandage. The bandage should be rolled up before you start. When rolling the bandage around the tail the roll should be on top of the bandage you are laying down so it looks a bit like a snail **(Fig. 58)**. Begin by unravelling about

Figure 58: The roll should be on top of the bandage that is being put down. Try to remember it should look like a snail.

25cm of bandage then lay it underneath the horse's tail as high up as you can go. Fold the short end of the bandage round to the front with the upper corner pulled upwards slightly. Secure this in position by rolling the bandage around over it then fold the corner that is sticking up down and bring the bandage around again to go over the corner you have just folded down. Continue to roll the bandage around and down the tail so the bandage you are placing down covers up half of the layer above it. Ideally you should bandage to the end of the tail bone then back up the tail until you run out. When you get to the end of the bandage tie the cords into a bow or fix it down if it is Velcro. A bow should ideally be to the side of the tail and tucked into the bandage to prevent the horse being able to rub it undone. Finish by gently bending the bandaged tail over your arm to reshape it.

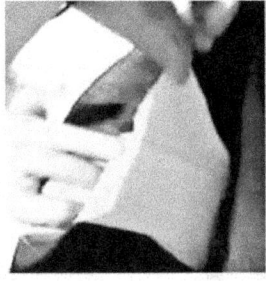 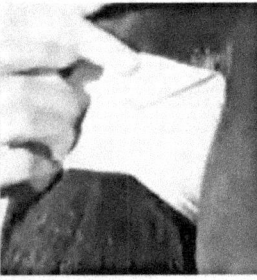 

Step 1: Lay the bandage flat high up under the horse's tail. Fold the end round to the front with the upper corner pulled upwards. Roll the bandage around once to secure in

Step 2: Fold the corner down and bring the bandage around again to go over the corner you have just folded down.

Step 3: Roll the bandage around and down the tail so the bandage you place down covers up half of the layer of bandage above it.

  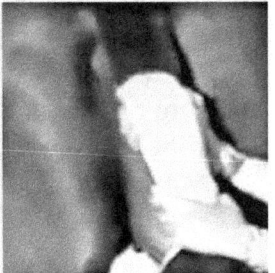

Step 4: Tie the two cords into a bow at the side of the tail or strap it down if it is Velcro. Tuck the bow into the bandage.

Step 5: Gently bend the bandaged tail over your arm to reshape it.

Step 6: Remove the bandage by undoing the cords and pulling the bandage down from the very top in one swift movement.

17. If plaiting, dampen the mane with a wet water brush and separate the mane into an odd number of equally sized sections (approximately 9) **(Fig 59)**.

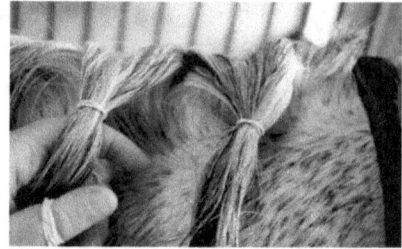

Figure 59: Dampen and divide the mane. Secure the sections with elastic bands.

18. Plait each section and fasten with a small elastic band. Put one plait in the forelock too.

19. Roll the plait up towards the underneath of the plait and secure it with another small elastic band. Do the same with the forelock **(Fig 60)**.

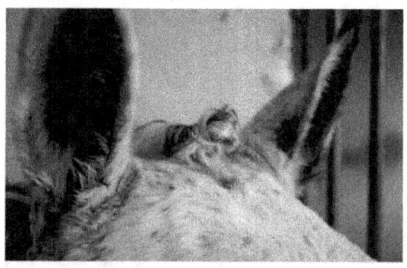

Figure 60: Don't forget to plait the forelock!

20. If you are plaiting the tail too then remove the tail bandage. The tail is normally plaited in the same way you would French plait someone's hair. If the horse is not being shown straight away then you may want to put the tail bandage back on over the plait to prevent the tail getting dirty. A big forelock can be French plaited too then rolled up.

Figure 61: Applying hoof oil to prevent hooves becoming brittle.

21. Give the horse's body a final wipe over with a stable rubber.

22. Apply hoof oil **(Fig. 61)**.

Bathing

If the horse is particularly muddy, stained or scurfy you may need to bath them first. This will make the grooming process easier and the horse will look and feel better for it too.

You will need the following to bath your horse:

⅄ A couple of buckets of warm water or a hosepipe connected to a mixer tap (**Fig 62**)

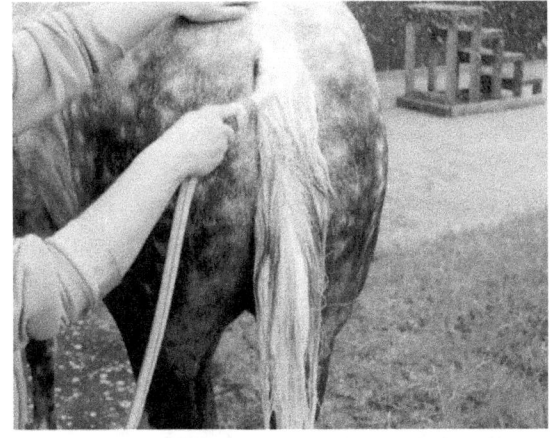

⅄ Sponge

⅄ Shampoo

⅄ Conditioner

Figure 62: There is nothing wrong with using a hosepipe on your horse providing they are happy with it and you can control the temperature.

⅄ Water brush

⅄ Sweat scraper

⅄ Hoof pick

⅄ A few towels

Some horses enjoy being bathed whereas others may be rather nervous of the idea. Be prepared for a jumpy or difficult horse and if the horse is good then great! If the horse does make a scene then at least you are prepared for it.

Tie the horse up outside or in an empty stable with a loose quick release knot. This way, if the horse panics and pulls back they can get away safely then you can catch and reassure them once they have calmed down (do make sure all gates are closed beforehand!). If the horse panics and the knot is tight and fails to give way the situation could escalate and the horse could end up injuring themselves and anyone nearby. If the horse is likely to fuss or fidget you can always tie a haynet up in front of them. This will distract the horse and keep them busy while you get the job done.

To bath a horse you will need to do the following:

1. Collect everything you need from the list above and put it where you can get to it but the horse cannot.

2. Lead the horse to where you intend to bath them and tie them up using a loose quick release knot.

3. Pick out the horse's feet and give them a scrub. Sweep away any mess. This helps to prevent dirty water splashing up the horse's legs.

4. Wet and lather up the horse's head, neck and mane **(Fig 63)**. Use a wet sponge for the face as some horses will object to have running water on their face. Avoid getting water in the horse's ears as this can really irritate them.

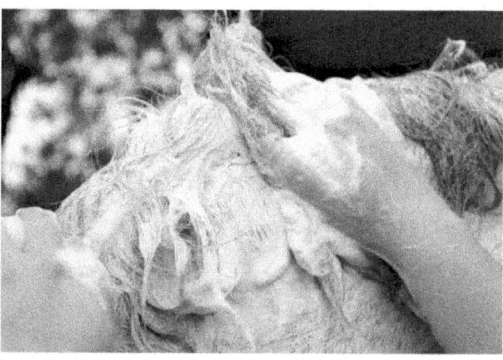

Figure 63: Washing the horse's mane.

5. Make your way back then down the horse's body. Wetting then lathering right down to the horse's fetlocks. Give the tail a good wash too as it can get particularly grubby! The

best way to wash the tail is to dunk it into a bucket of warm water then lather it up.

6. Rinse the horse's head, neck and mane with clean, warm water. Again, use a sponge for the face. Rub your fingers over the horse's hair to make sure there is no shampoo left.

7. Squeeze out any excess water from the mane and use a sweat scraper to remove any excess water from the neck. The best way to use the scraper is to place it at the highest point then scrape back or down in the direction the hair is laying. This tool should not be used on the face.

8. Now thoroughly rinse off the rest of the horse starting at the highest point working your way down. Rinse the tail by dunking it back into a bucket of clean warm water. Remove any remaining suds by pouring clean, warm water over the tail at its highest point.

9. Use the sweat scraper to remove any excess water from the body. Start from the top and work your way back and down. Do not use this tool on the horse's legs.

10. Squeeze the water out of the horse's tail then spin it (a bit like helicopter rotor blades). This will help remove water from the tail.

11. Give the horse a good rub down with a towel to dry them off as best as possible.

If you are going to go straight on to grooming the horse to prepare them for the show make sure the horse has been properly dried first. You can walk them around a bit to help them warm up and dry off if needs be. Some yards will even have a solarium which is like a stable with heat lamps. Standing the horse in here will dry them off quickly and easily.

If the horse is being bathed the day before the show you will need to apply a tail bandage to prevent the tail getting dirty overnight. Rug the horse up to help keep them warm. If they are still damp then be sure to change the rug after an hour so they are not standing around in a damp rug (these rugs must be clean!). Apply stable bandages to all four legs to prevent them getting dirty overnight. Be aware though that bandaging over damp legs may make the hair curly.

How to apply stable bandages / polo wraps:

1. Brush the leg down with a body brush to remove dirt and bedding.

2. Wrap a piece of fibre gee, gam gee or neoprene dressing around the leg, making sure there are no creases and the ends are not resting over the horse's tendons. The dressing should cover the knee or hock and at least cover the coronary band.

3. Place the bandage just below the knee or hock with the top corner pointing up slightly.

4. Wrap the bandage around twice in a clockwise direction to secure the bandage in place. The roll should be on top so it looks like a snail.

5. Fold the corner down and wrap the bandage back around to secure it.

6. Wrap the bandage around and down the leg so each layer you put down covers the lower half of the layer above it.

7. Bandage down to just underneath the ergot then bandage back up the leg. Aim to create an upside down V at the bottom to the front of the leg when changing direction. This offers a bit of give and helps to prevent the bottom of the bandage scrunching up.

8. If possible, the bandage should be secured in place on the outside of the horse's leg. Polo wraps and stable bandages usually fasten with Velcro.

9. Slide one finger between the bandage and the horse's leg at the top of the bandage. You should be able to do this comfortably. If the bandage is too tight it can damage the horse's tendons. If it is too loose it can come off and become hazardous.

10. To remove – Undo the Velcro and unwind the bandage quickly by passing it from hand to hand. Remove the dressing if used. Finally, give the leg a gentle rub down to increase circulation then roll the bandage back up.

Polo wraps are applied in the same way but without the first layer of dressing. They are used to support the horse's legs during exercise whereas stable bandages are used to protect the horse's legs and also offer support, warmth and help control swelling.

Safety Tips

The hosepipe should be out of the way so it cannot be tripped over and you should check that the water is not too hot before using it on the horse.

Keep your work area tidy to prevent tripping hazards. This will make it easier to work around the horse too!

Remember to stand to the side when doing anything behind the horse in case they kick out.

If the horse is objecting to washing or rinsing then avoid forcing it on them. Stop, reassure then try again slowly and gently. If the horse is having none of it go and ask for help.

Cleanliness

It is good practice to clean your bathing and grooming tools. This should be done roughly after each use and thoroughly about once every couple of weeks. Hair should be removed from brushes and dust shaken out for a quick clean. This makes the tools usable and effective for the next use. When cleaning thoroughly you should do the same again but also scrub all of the tools in hot, soapy water and rinse them off in a disinfecting solution such as hibiscrub. This prevents the build-up of bacteria and stops spreading dirt and germs to your horse.

Each horse should have their own grooming kit used only for them. This may sound excessive but it will prevent the spread of infections such as ring worm. This could become quite a problem if there is an outbreak on a busy yard as it could put horses out of use and reduce the income to the business.

The Role of the Groom

If you are taking your own horse to a show by yourself you will have quite a job on your hands as there is quite a lot that will need to be done...more than you might think! Not only do you have to prepare your horse for the show as previously described but you will also have to prepare yourself and the transport then warm up and cool down your horse before and after competing. Then you have to prepare the horse for travelling again, get back home and get the horse comfortable. You may want to take a friend or family member with you to give you a helping hand. This can help to take a load off when you have to stay focused and in control for the competition itself.

The following is a schedule of everything that needs to be done before, during and after the show. This is what would be expected of a competition groom and therefore if you took your own horse to a show by yourself this is what you would have to do.

To Do List

Day Before Show

1) Bath Oscar

2) Give Oscar a thorough groom

3) Check Oscar is sound

4) Clean tack thoroughly

5) Check show numnahs and bandages are clean and dry

6) Check trailer / lorry is clean and safe

7) Check lorry / towing vehicle starts

8) Check petrol, oil, water, tyre pressure, tyre tread

9) Check I have all the correct paperwork

10) Attach bailing twine to securing rings

11) Put food, filled haynets and water containers in lorry

12) Put spare rugs in lorry

13) Put bedding down on lorry / trailer floor

14) Plan route and pack a map

Morning of Show

1) *Muck out*

2) *Feed Oscar*

3) *Check Oscar is still sound*

4) *Remove any stains on Oscar*

5) *Groom*

6) *Plait up mane and tail*

7) *Bandage tail*

8) *Apply hoof oil*

9) *Make sure brushes are clean*

10) *Get myself ready*

Things to put in lorry

- *Tack*
- *Boots and bandages*
- *Grooming kit*
- *Spare plaiting kit*
- *Equine first aid kit (check everything is present first)*
- *Skip, shovel and broom*
- *2-3 buckets*
- *Steps (for plaiting)*
- *Lunge Line and whip*
- *Shampoo*
- *Several large, dry towels*

During Show

1) Go to show reception. Show papers and collect number
2) Find out if show is on time
3) Find out where to go and when
4) Remove Oscars travel gear and tidy him up
5) Tack Oscar up
6) Throw rug over Oscar if it is cold
7) Lead Oscar around for 15 minutes
8) Help rider get on Oscar
9) Be ready to help rider when needed
10) Help rider dismount
11) Walk Oscar around for 15 minutes
12) Untack Oscar and sponge him down
13) Offer water and hay to Oscar
14) Groom and unplait mane and tail
15) Rug Oscar up if it is cold
16) Prepare Oscar for travelling

After Show

1) Unload Oscar and remove travel gear
2) Give Oscar a quick brush over and put in stable
3) Make sure Oscar has hay and water
4) Remove everything from lorry that we travelled with
5) Muck out lorry
6) Lock up lorry and put everything away
7) Give tack a quick clean

Types of Competitions

Dressage

The dressage rider **(Fig. 64)** performs manoeuvres on the horse in the form of a test in front of a judge. The rider needs to be able to show effortless control of the horse and show that the horse is listening to their aids. These manoeuvres were originally developed for riders going into battle on horses. Soldiers used their horse as a weapon and advanced the horse in a way that would help them fight and intimidate the enemy.

Figure 64: Competing in dressage.

Dressage competitions are either affiliated or unaffiliated. Affiliated competitions have strict rules that must be adhered to by grooms, riders and course builders. This ensures that these competitions are as safe and as fair as possible. Unaffiliated competitions are not as strict and are more likely to be held at your local yard.

Figure 65: Competing in jumping.

Riders complete affiliated dressage tests to score points. This allows them to start from the bottom and work their way up to more challenging tests.

Show Jumping

Riders that wish to compete at show jumping **(Fig. 65)** also have a choice of whether to go affiliated or unaffiliated. The rider must complete a course of jumps in the correct order with as few refusals or jumps knocked down as possible. In this case, unlike dressage, the less points the better.

Jumping originated from riders hunting foxes. They needed their horses to jump walls and fences that had been erected to mark the boundaries of people's properties.

Cross Country

Cross country is where a rider rides their horse around an outdoor course that involves jumping over obstacles **(Fig. 66)**. The rules are similar to show jumping in that the rider must try to avoid refusals and falling off. The obstacles cannot really be knocked down so the horse must clearly jump over the obstacles and be on the correct side of the flag at the site of the jump.

Figure 66: Competing in cross country.

Eventing

Eventing is where a horse and rider must compete at dressage, show jumping and cross country all in one event. These events can last for up to three days so the horse needs to be fit and prepared beforehand and the rider and groom should come well equipped. All three disciplines need to be attempted and the overall method of scoring is points based.

In-Hand Showing

In-hand showing is where a horse is shown off for their looks and conformation. The horse is not ridden; instead, they are lead around **(Fig. 67)** and must walk and trot up in front of the judges. They are scored on overall presentation, conformation and control. The horse must be well groomed according to their breed type and they should act on command.

Figure 67: Competing at in-hand showing.

Driving

Carriage driving is not as popular as the other forms of competitions today. It is something that is still practised in various forms and there are some shows that take place for driving.

Figure 68: Scurrying.

Smaller, more agile ponies are used more for scurrying **(Fig. 68)**. This is where a single pony up to a team of ponies will pull a lightweight exercise cart around a slalom of cones with a ball balanced on top of each.

The balls must stay on top of the cones and the aim is to complete the course in the fastest time possible.

Larger horses are used more for cross country. As with scurrying, a single horse or a team of horses **(Fig. 69)** can be used to pull the cart around an outdoor course. The course is similar to the ridden cross country course although obviously the driving horses are not expected to jump! They must be guided around a course of

Figure 69: Cross country with a team of 4 horses.

obstacles, winding pathways and through water.

Racing

Racing is aimed at smaller framed people mainly because the horse must gallop as fast as possible and they can do this better when carrying less weight. The saddle and even the horse's shoes

Figure 70: Race horses jumping a fence during a steeple chase race.

are super lightweight all so that they can go faster. Different countries have their own take on racing but the most common style of racing is either to gallop a set distance and the rider who finishes first wins or the horse must jump over fences **(Fig. 70)** during the race (steeple chasing). The horse is not penalised for touching the hedging when jumping over it though some horses unfortunately do not make it to the end of the race as they sometimes fall at these fences. This is because a horse will struggle to gain height if they are travelling too fast.

Transportation

While transporting horses there are a lot of things that need to be taken into consideration. It is not just a case of throwing the horse in the back of a trailer and off you go. You need to make sure that the transportation is safe, suitable and can cope with the weight of the horse. The horse will need to wear protective clothing to help prevent knocks, bumps, rubbing and grazes and you will need to put things in the horse's immediate environment to keep him comfortable and occupied. You will also need to take a route that is as straight as possible and suitable for larger, slower vehicles.

Types of Transport

Larger yards that transport horses regularly usually have a horse lorry **(Fig. 71)**. This allows the transportation of several horses all at once and there is storage space and sometimes even a sleeping area for people too!

Figure 71: A horse lorry.

Figure 72: A horse trailer being towed by a vehicle of a sufficient size.

If transportation is only needed for one or two horses then a trailer **(Fig. 72)** is used. This is obviously a lot smaller than a horse lorry and does not provide much storage space. These trailers are not suitable for heavier horses whereas a horse box **(Fig. 73)** may be more appropriate. This is smaller than a lorry and will transport a couple of heavy horses with storage space too. Unfortunately, these horse boxes do not normally have sleeping areas for people like the lorries do.

Figure 73: A horse box.

Horse lorries are generally more expensive due to their sheer size and accessories. Horse boxes are cheaper but be wary if buying cheap second hand ones. These may be unsafe to transport horses due to excessive use or lack of care. Horse trailers are obviously cheaper again as they are small and less equipped. They are more commonly used on small yards or by people who have one or two horses because they are cheaper, take up less space and do the job. Again, cheap older ones may be unsafe. Do check them thoroughly for safety. Look out especially for rotten flooring.

Vehicle Checks

Whether you are looking to buy horse transportation or are just about to use your existing transportation it is so important to check the whole vehicle or trailer for safety and road usability. This is because when accidents happen involving horse transportation they are usually quite horrific. Below is a list of all the things you should check, whatever type of transport you are using.

Figure 74: Inside a horse trailer. If only one horse is being transported load them into the right hand side to help balance the trailer. This is because the trailer will lean to the left a little due to the camber of the road.

General Safety

- ⚔ Check the floor on which the horse will be standing is not rotten. Look under any rubber matting. Have a good jump around on it if you want to!

- ⚔ Check there are no sharp edges on any walls, partitions or gates.

- ⚔ Check breakable string is attached to the securing rings for the horse to be tied up to. (This is so the horse can break free if needs be. The ring itself will not give).

- ⚔ Check the ramp is clean and sturdy **(Fig. 74)**, not muddy or rotten. It should not dip in the middle and there should be no nails or sharp objects sticking up.

- ⚔ Check the windows are not cracked or broken. Check they are operable.

- ⚔ Check all partitions move freely and securely lock into place when put into position. Make sure they offer enough room for the horse but not too much that it could cause them to lose their balance.

- ⚔ Check the ramp locks securely into position when it is put back up. It should open and close easily.

- ⚔ The environment should be clean. It should not be dusty, mucky or full of cob webs.

Vehicle Checks

- Check there is enough engine oil in the lorry, horse box or towing vehicle. The oil level can be found on the dipstick where the oil is poured into the engine.

- Check the water level. This should be somewhere between the maximum and minimum lines. If it is at minimum you may want to top it up before leaving.

- Check there is enough fuel by turning the engine on and looking at the gauge on the dash board.

- Check all of the lights work. You will need to test the brake lights, reverse lights, fog lights, tail lights, head lights (dipped and full beam) and all indicators. If you cannot see any when testing them get someone to watch while you test them. You should not take any vehicle on the road when a bulb is not working so make sure to replace any that aren't. If you are using a trailer then the rear lights should be linked up to the towing vehicle and these should all work too.

- Check the horn sounds properly.

- Check the wipers work and the washers spray water. There should be plenty of water in the washer bottle.

- Check the tyre pressure in each tyre. Pump up any soft tyres beforehand if possible or go to a petrol station to pump the tyres up, preferably before loading the horse(s).

- Check there are no cracks, bulges or invasive objects in the tyres.

- Check the tread of the tyres is at least 1.6mm in depth across at least three quarters of the tread.

- Check there is a spare tyre present that is in good condition and blown up. If you are towing a trailer there should be a spare tyre for the trailer and a spare tyre for the towing vehicle.

Journey Preparations

The holding area of the transport is usually prepared quite
similarly to a stable. Some floors will have rubber matting to help
give the horse grip whereas some floors are standard with bedding
on top. In all cases there should be fresh bedding present for the
horse to stand on so they are comfortable and happy to urinate if
the need should arise. There should be a haynet hung up for the
horse to eat to keep them busy and distracted while travelling.
This should ideally be right in front of the horse or tied to the
same ring they are tied to to prevent them straining to get to it
(Fig. 75).

*Figure 75: A horse in transport with a
haynet to keep him occupied.*

It can get quite warm in
the holding area once you
have loaded the horse(s)
so ventilation is a must.
Lorries and horse boxes
have little windows high
up that can be opened to
let hot air out and
sometimes there is a fan
to help circulate the air.
Trailers have a top door
that can be opened which
allows hot air out and
cool air in though this may not be usable if the horse is jumpy or
not used to travelling. If it is particularly hot then it may be better
to travel at night if possible.

Long journeys will require some planning ahead. You may need
to stop off somewhere overnight to allow the horse to rest
properly and to refresh yourself and anyone travelling with you.
You will need to stop every three to four hours to allow the horse
to drink. If the horse is known to avoid water while travelling then
you can try soaking the haynet. This way the horse is getting
water during the journey. Offering carrots during pit stops will

also help as they are tasty treats and full of water. Adding sugar beet to the horse's feed will also help to prevent the horse from becoming dehydrated. The horse should not be given hard feed while the transport is in motion as the movement and bumping around could cause him to choke. During the pit stops you should check the bedding to see if the horse has urinated. If he has not then you could try turning the engine off. The noise and bumping around may have been putting him off! Remove any droppings during pit stops too to make the horse more comfortable.

If the horse is normally worked regularly you should exercise him as normal if this is possible while on a stopover. This is because if the horse has a build-up of nutrients and nothing to do with them he could develop a painful condition called azoturia. Also, the lack of freedom to move around could cause colic.

Plan Your Route!

Whether your journey is going to be long or short you should always take a quick look at a map **(Fig. 76)** beforehand to make sure you are taking the best route to suit the horse and vehicle. Your route should be as straight as possible

Figure 76: A compass and map - particularly useful if you get lost!

with as few roundabouts as possible and the roads should be big enough to take your transport.

Imagine having to stand up on a bus while travelling to your destination. You may have a handle or a pole to hold on to which you may find yourself grabbing for when the bus goes around bends and roundabouts. The horse is in the same situation in the trailer or lorry only they do not have the option to hold onto anything. They can shift their weight, pull back on the lead rope a bit or lean against a wall or partition if their weight is being shifted but it can still be a wobbly journey for them. This is why it is best to take a nice straight road whenever possible. Main roads such as 'A' roads and motorways **(Fig. 77)** are therefore the best option as they are usually bigger and fairly straight with fewer obstacles. 'B' roads are usually narrow and wiggly **(Fig. 78)** and can be bumpier for the horse. It can sometimes become difficult when passing oncoming vehicles too. There are usually horses being ridden, cyclists or walkers around as well which will make driving more difficult. Smaller roads can also come with weight limits, low bridges, low hanging branches, speed bumps and blind bends – none of which are suitable for larger vehicles.

Figure 77: A motorway or 'A' road is the best road to choose for travelling on. It is open, offers good visibility and a lot of the time offers a slow lane so faster traffic can overtake you without making the situation dangerous.

Figure 78: Try to avoid 'B' roads, country roads and driving through towns. Visibility is usually limited, the roads are winding, not as well kept and sudden dangers can spring up without much warning.

The best way to plan a route is either by using a paper map and looking for the best route and noting down the directions (take the map with you too!) or use a map on the internet. There are plenty of websites that will generate a route for you if you give your starting point and your destination. You can even state whether you prefer a straight route, a quick route or a short route. You can then print these directions and the map out and take them with you.

Sat Navs are helpful when trying to find your way around but they should probably be avoided if possible when transporting horses as they can take you down roads that are perhaps not suitable for larger vehicles or trailers or they may lead you to a dead end and turning around could be difficult. If you do need to use a Sat Nav look at the route it has planned for you first to make sure it looks suitable. Whatever method you choose to use make sure the map is up to date!

Travel Clothing

Once you have prepared the transport for the horse and you have your route ready you then need to prepare the horse for travelling. The horse will need travel clothing which will help to protect them from knocks, bumps and grazes during the journey – especially if the horse is difficult to load and is likely to rear up or jump around a bit. Not all items of protective clothing will be needed in all cases but it is best if the horse's head, legs and tail are protected at all times. All of the clothing has advantages and disadvantages so it is best to consider the horse that will be travelling then decide what will be best to wrap them up in.

Clothing	Advantages	Disadvantages
Leather head collar	⅄ Looks smart and presentable ⅄ Will break if the horse needs to pull free in an emergency ⅄ Comfortable for the horse ⅄ Easy to clean	⅄ More expensive to buy than nylon head collars ⅄ Need to be cleaned, oiled and looked after unlike nylon ones
<td colspan="3">Reason for use: Allows the horse to be secured and lead on and off the vehicle.</td>

Poll guard 	⅄ Protects the horse's head if they rear up and bang their head while loading or unloading ⅄ Easy to attach to head collar ⅄ Stays in place	⅄ Difficult to put on a head shy horse ⅄ It can make the horse hot and sweaty ⅄ It can rub the forelock or plait and make it scruffy
Reason for use: This protects the horse's poll should the horse spook while loading or unloading. Rearing in the holding area can cause nasty head injuries and even death.		
Travel boots 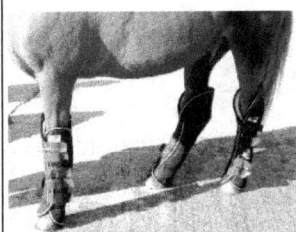	⅄ Quick and easy to apply ⅄ Give plenty of protection all around the leg ⅄ Offer more padding than bandages ⅄ Over reach boots are not needed as they go down to the floor	⅄ Velcro becomes less effective over time ⅄ Velcro may frighten a young horse ⅄ Can irritate the horse and cause sweating ⅄ Do not support legs ⅄ Hard to get a good fit ⅄ May slip down
Reason for use: The padding protects a large portion of the legs all around from superficial injuries caused by spooking or loss of balance while travelling.		

Travel pads and bandages 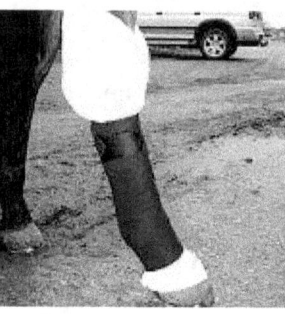	⋏ Stretchy and easy to apply securely ⋏ Offer more support to legs than travel boots ⋏ Light weight ⋏ Easy to fit ⋏ Wash and dry easily	⋏ Take longer to put on ⋏ Dangerous if they come undone ⋏ Can damage muscles if put on incorrectly ⋏ Take a while to remove and roll ⋏ Additional protection may be needed

Reason for use: Bandaging the horse's leg will support and protect the area it covers and help to prevent swelling from occurring.

Over reach boots 	⋏ Durable and hard wearing ⋏ Cannot slip down out of position	⋏ Aging Velcro can become less effective ⋏ Pull on boots can be awkward to put on ⋏ Must fit well ⋏ May cause the horse to trip (more likely if they are the wrong size)

Reason for use: These protect the front feet if the back feet move too far forward and clip them. This could happen if the horse moves around a lot in the holding area or has to quickly rebalance.

Travel knee and hock boots  	⋏ Offer protection when the horse is shifting their weight in the lorry ⋏ Help to keep the legs cooler ⋏ Easier to clean than travel boots	⋏ Do not protect the whole leg ⋏ Can restrict horse's movement ⋏ May rub and cause sores

Reason for use: These offer protection to the front of the knee and the back of the hock. These areas are more likely to obtain superficial injuries while travelling.

Tail bandage 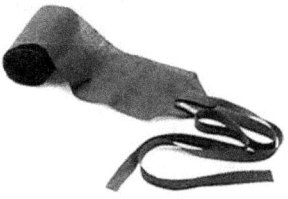	⋏ Looks tidy ⋏ Fits firmly in place ⋏ Stops horse rubbing tail on the bar ⋏ Helps to keep the tail clean	⋏ Cannot protect above its highest point ⋏ Can damage tail if applied too tight ⋏ Takes a while to put on ⋏ May come undone ⋏ Securing knot may rub the tail

Reason for use: The bandage prevents the horse rubbing his tail on the bar behind him in the holding area. This prevents injury and preserves the hair or plait.

Tail guard 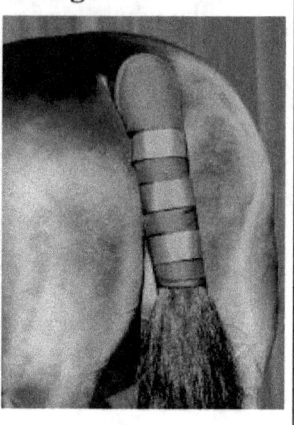	⅄ Cannot be applied too tightly ⅄ Easy to put on ⅄ Protects above its highest wrap around point ⅄ Can go over a tail bandage	⅄ Can be tricky to fasten and to get all of the hair in and flat ⅄ Can slip down ⅄ Not all tail guards cover the whole dock

Reason for use: The tail guard prevents the horse rubbing its tail on the bar behind them in the holding area. It can also prevent injury from knocks as they are usually well padded. The hair or plait is also preserved and kept tidy.

Cotton summer sheet 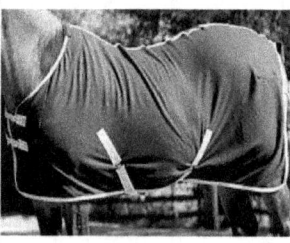	⅄ Light weight, cool and breathable ⅄ Not itchy ⅄ Keeps the breeze off the horse ⅄ Will not cause the horse to get too warm ⅄ Inexpensive	⅄ Does not offer much protection ⅄ Does not allow sweat to escape ⅄ Damages easily

Reason for use: This rug will keep dust and draughts off the horse on a hot day.

Thermatex rug	⅄ Keeps the horse warm ⅄ Looks smart ⅄ Lets the sweat get out ⅄ Can be layered with more rugs if it is particularly cold	⅄ Too warm to use in summer ⅄ Expensive
Reason for use: Keeps dust off the horse and helps to keep them warm on cooler days.		
Wool Newmarket rug	⅄ Looks smart and tidy ⅄ Keeps the horse warm ⅄ Breathable	⅄ Expensive ⅄ Difficult to wash ⅄ Itchy ⅄ Can be heavy ⅄ Can retain odours
Reason for use: Keeps dust off the horse and keeps them warm while looking smart.		
Lightweight fleece rug	⅄ Washes and dries easily ⅄ Looks smart ⅄ Inexpensive ⅄ Helps take sweat away from horse	⅄ Not warm enough for winter use ⅄ Not very robust ⅄ Not waterproof ⅄ Bedding sticks to them making them look untidy
Reason for use: Keeps dust and draughts off the horse and allows sweat out if the horse gets hot.		

Roller and breast girth 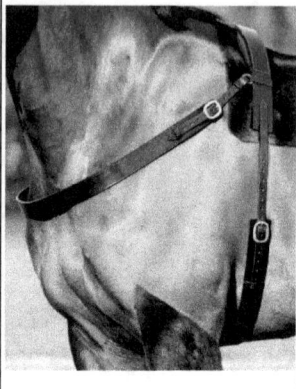	⅄ Keeps rugs securely in place ⅄ Can attach to tail guard to prevent it slipping down ⅄ Prevents you having to bend down ⅄ Horse cannot get legs caught up like with surcingles ⅄ Does not press down on the spine	⅄ Horse could be more likely to get themselves caught on something ⅄ Can be done up too tight ⅄ Expensive ⅄ Heavy for the horse

<u>Reason for use</u>: Used instead of surcingles to rule out the risk of them coming loose and the horse getting their legs tangled in them. Layered rugs can all be fastened up together securely so there is one girth rather than a collection of surcingles.

Cooler sheet 	⅄ Ideal for summer use ⅄ Easy to wash ⅄ Breathable ⅄ Can be layered	⅄ Horse can get caught on things easily and cause damage to the rug

<u>Reason for use</u>: Keeps the draught off the horse and allows sweat to escape, enabling the horse to keep cool.

Going Further

Tack

Types of Saddle

There are many types of saddle around the world and some countries have their own style of saddle for casual riding. A good example of this is the ornate American western saddle **(Fig. 80)**. The well-known saddle for English casual riding is called the general purpose saddle **(Fig. 79)**. It allows you to ride in all disciplines but it is not designed to aid any specific discipline. For this reason some event riders choose to use the general purpose saddle because it is a compromise between a dressage and a jumping saddle. The saddle flaps are long enough to allow for a longer stirrup length used for dressage but they are also forward to allow for and support the leg in a shorter stirrup for jumping. The seat is deep so that the dressage rider can sit comfortably but the pommel and cantle are not as high as they are on the dressage saddle. This is to allow room for movement while jumping.

Figure 79: A typical general purpose saddle.

Figure 80: A typical western style saddle.

If you want to specialise in a certain discipline then using appropriate tack designed for that sport will help you.

Dressage

A dressage saddle **(Fig. 81)** allows you to sit deep into the seat of the saddle which helps the rider to remain comfortable. The front of the saddle flap is sometimes stuffed to remind the rider to keep a long leg. The rider can use their legs more effectively to instruct the horse because the girth straps are usually longer and therefore the girth is not hindering the aids the rider is trying to give. Overall, the saddle aims to encourage a better riding position without obstructing the rider.

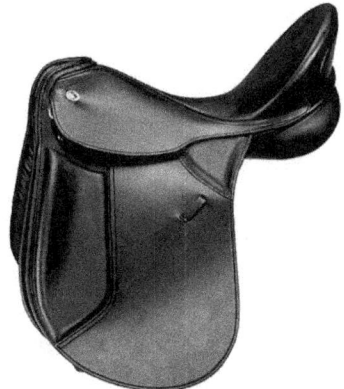

Figure 81: A typical dressage saddle.

Jumping

The jumping saddle **(Fig. 82)** also aims to assist with the riding position, providing the rider adopts the correct position. The pommel and cantle of the jumping saddle are lower which allows the rider to take up the forward jumping position. They also have more room to lean back for jumping into water or riding down slopes. The flaps of the saddle are shorter and

Figure 82: A typical jumping saddle.

are more forward. This allows the rider to have shorter stirrups which are needed for jumping. The knee roll is more defined to help support the knee while riding.

Racing

The racing saddle **(Fig. 83)** is extremely small and light – some weighing as little as 8 ounces. This is because the horse can gallop faster with less weight on their back. The seat is long and flat with very little padding underneath. This is to allow the rider as much room to move as possible so they can stand up and forward in the racing position and briefly sit down while

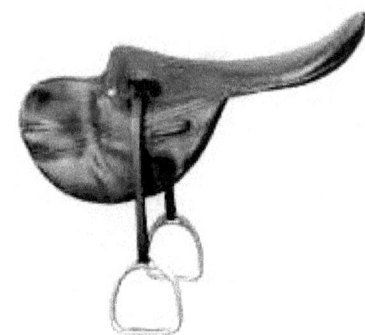

Figure 83: A typical racing saddle.

they are not racing. The saddle flaps are extremely short to allow for the very short stirrups the rider will have. The saddle does not protect the horse's spine like other saddles as it is built on a half tree. This is tolerable because the rider spends most of their time off the seat anyway but for this reason the racing saddle should not be used for casual riding.

Types of Bridle

Snaffle Bridle

The snaffle bridle **(Fig. 84)** is used for casual riding and can be used for all types of riding. It allows good control of the horse and is not too harsh on the horse's nose. There are many variations to parts of the bridle which cater for different types and levels of horse. Parts such as the bit and the noseband come in many different styles and provide various actions, all of which can be fitted

Figure 84: A snaffle bridle with a cavesson noseband and loose ring snaffle bit.

onto most bridles. The snaffle bridle normally consists of a cavesson noseband and a snaffle bit though the bit can be changed to suit the horse and rider.

Pelham Bridle

The pelham bridle **(Fig. 85)** is made up similarly to the snaffle bridle but it has a pelham bit which is controlled by two sets of reins. The snaffle rein allows the rider to control the horse like the reins on a normal snaffle bridle. The curb rein pulls on the shanks which engage the curb chain. This pulls the chin in and exerts pressure on the horse's poll, causing the horse to round its neck. There is more leverage because of the shanks (which can vary in length) so more pressure is exerted on the horse's mouth. For this reason the rider must be gentle with the reins and the horse will hopefully become more responsive to the bit with less rein action needed from the rider.

Figure 85: A pelham bridle with a snaffle rein (top) and a curb rein (bottom).

If a rider needs the control that the pelham bit gives but does not want to hold two sets of reins then pelham roundings **(Fig. 86)** can be used which enable you to control the bit and the curb chain with one set of reins (if you are competing, make sure these are actually allowed first!). This type of bridle can be used for most disciplines. Its purpose is to allow lots of control over the horse without having to use too

Figure 86: An example of a pair of roundings. One end attaches to the bit ring and the other end attaches to the ring on the shank to provide a loop for one set of reins to attach to. The bit becomes less effective when it is controlled this way.

much rein. Horses that get a bit strong may need a pelham bridle to help the rider steady the horse.

Double Bridle

The double bridle **(Fig. 87)** is similar to the pelham bridle in that it has snaffle and curb action but it actually has two bits. The bits are generally smaller and are both controlled with a separate set of reins. The smaller snaffle bit is called the bradoon and the curb bit is called the Weymouth bit. This bridle is normally used in dressage and in some dressage competitions (Prix St Georges and above) it is compulsory for the horse to wear one. The bits allow the rider to give more complex instructions to the horse and the curb action allows the rider to collect the horse which is why it is preferred in advanced dressage.

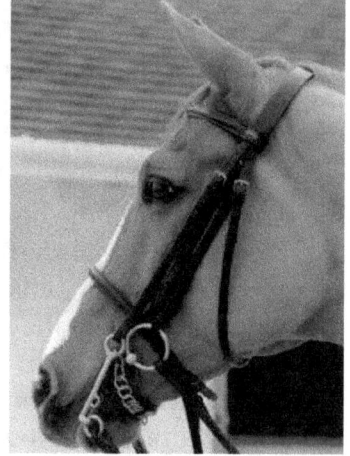

Figure 87: A double bridle. Notice the two separate bits.

Hackamore

The hackamore **(Fig. 88)** is a bitless bridle which allows the rider to instruct the horse by exerting pressure on the nose, chin and poll. There are many variations to the bitless bridle but the mechanical hackamore is more common in the UK. This type of hackamore, although bitless, carries a

Figure 88: A hackamore bridle.

shank and curb chain. For this reason the rider must still be gentle with the reins or this bridle could become dangerous in the wrong hands. The horse cannot be steered through this bridle so the rider needs to use their legs and body to direct the horse. The hackamore is more suited to an experienced rider and a horse that will not accept a bit or has a mouth injury.

<u>Gag</u>

The gag **(Fig. 89)** causes the horse to lift their head and pull it in. This is useful with a horse that leans on the bit or gets excited and pulls. Some variations of the gag require two sets of reins for control. One set of reins control the snaffle action while the second set engage the gag action which exerts pressure on the horse's lips and poll.

Figure 89: A gag bridle with a Cheltenham gag bit.

Disciplines such as eventing, jumping and polo allow the use of a gag bit because the rider needs to be able to maintain control of the horse and compete safely and these particular sports, risky as they are, become more dangerous if the horse has a tendency to run away with the rider. The gag is not permitted for use in dressage as it has the opposite effect of what the rider is trying to achieve. In dressage the horse must show obedience, a good outline and be on the bit. The gag prevents or masks all of these things.

Figure 90: A cavesson noseband.

Nosebands

Nosebands are not always needed but they can help to keep the horse from opening their mouth wide and trying to get their tongue over the bit to avoid pressure from it. A number of different types of nosebands are available – some are gentle or provide decoration only whereas others provide an action to help control the horse without having to exchange the bit for something more severe.

Cavesson

The standard riding bridle usually has a cavesson noseband **(Fig. 90)**. It is gentle on the horse's nose and provides a simple action which is to keep the horse from opening their mouth wide and getting their tongue over the bit. It can also be used if a standing martingale is needed as this needs to be attached to a noseband.

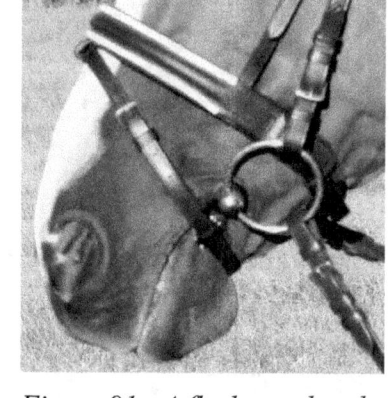

Figure 91: A flash noseband.

Flash

The flash noseband **(Fig. 91)** is the same as a cavesson but with an extra band that goes around the nose lower down. This helps to keep the horse's mouth closed if the noseband alone is not enough. The flash is used on horses that cross their jaw or prefer the bit to stay still in their mouth.

Grackle

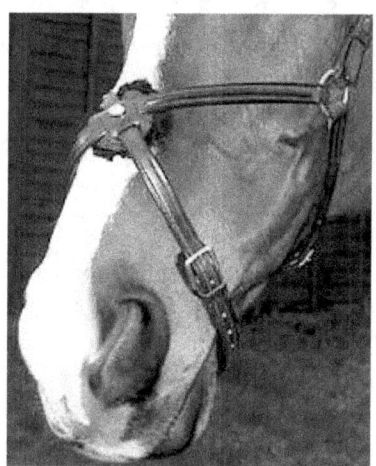

Figure 92: A grackle noseband.

The grackle **(Fig. 92)** is similar to the flash noseband in that it helps to prevent the horse from crossing its jaw or opening its mouth. It is more comfortable for the horse to wear and allows the horse's nostrils to expand more therefore being more useful for fast paced riding.

Drop

The drop noseband **(Fig. 93)** is like a flash without the cavesson. It helps to keep the horse's mouth closed which in turn helps to prevent the horse crossing their jaw. This noseband should not really be used for fast paced work as it can restrict the nostrils, especially if it has not been fitted properly. A standing martingale should not be used with this noseband because if the horse tried to lift their head the martingale will pull the noseband down against the nostrils and could cause the horse to panic.

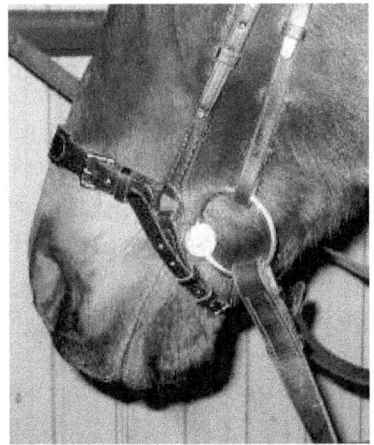

Figure 93: A drop noseband.

Kineton

The kineton **(Fig. 94)** is a severe noseband because it enforces bit action. The noseband does not encircle the whole nose but rather it sits on top of the nose lower down - midway between where a cavesson and a drop noseband would sit. At either end of the noseband there are metal semi-circular attachments that, once fitted to the horse, sit underneath the bit rings. A snaffle bit is used with this noseband and the semi-circular attachments intensify the feel of the bit rings on the horse's lips. This gives a rider more control over a strong horse without having to be heavy handed on the reins or having to use a more severe bit.

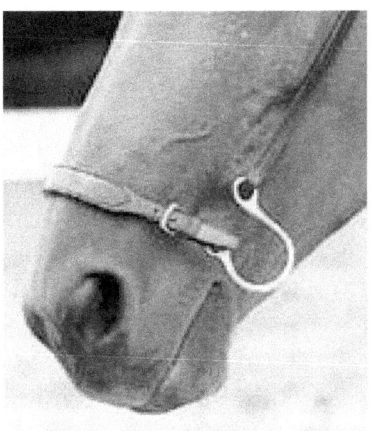

Figure 94: A kineton noseband.

Combination

The combination noseband **(Fig. 95)** is more severe as it can hurt the horse by pushing the cheeks in towards the molars. This noseband is similar to the kineton as there are two semi-circular pieces of metal that sit under the bit rings. One strap goes over the horse's nose just below where the cavesson would sit and two straps go under the horse's jaw. One of these sits in the chin groove and the other one is positioned just above where the cavesson noseband would fasten. Its

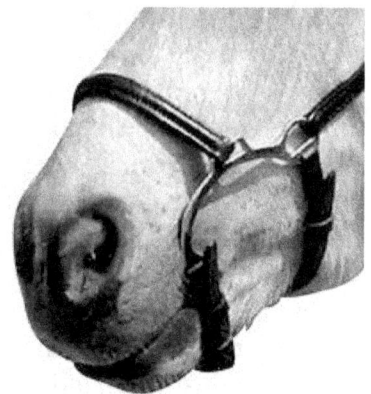

Figure 95: A combination noseband.

purpose is to put the horse off crossing their jaw which is accomplished by the metal semi-circular attachments. The noseband is similar to the grackle because of its action and pressure points though it does not hold the bit firmly in place.

Bits

There is a large variety of bits available all of which vary in severity and provide different actions to make a horse more manageable for the rider. As with all tack, countries will have their own versions and styles of bits but their aim is usually to produce similar reactions from the horse.

The snaffle bit is the most common and widely used bit due to many of them being gentle on the horse's mouth (although some types of snaffle can be more severe). The action of the snaffle is to put direct pressure on the horse's mouth without leverage. The areas under pressure can change according to the type of mouth piece and rings used. For this reason there are many types of snaffle.

The curb bit provides leverage. A double bridle uses a curb bit, known as a Weymouth bit, to provide leverage and another bit, known as the bradoon, to provide snaffle action. A pelham gives the rider snaffle and curb action but only one bit is needed. Two sets of reins are needed with a pelham bit – one to control the snaffle action and one to control the leverage. The snaffle reins attach to the bit rings for the rider to direct the horse and the curb reins attach to the shanks for the rider to control the horse's outline and sometimes speed and sensitivity. The leverage, provided by the shanks, allows the rider to ask the horse to flex and bring their head in to round the neck. This is done by applying pressure to the poll and chin groove. The chin groove is manipulated by use of a curb chain which is tightened when the curb rein is used. The mouthpiece can vary like with the snaffle to focus pressure on the tongue, bars and sometimes the roof of the mouth. A bit that has a port (a raised area at the centre of the mouthpiece) gives the tongue some relief but may put pressure on the roof of the mouth. A lower port can avoid contact with the roof of the mouth altogether whereas a high port can come into contact with the roof of the mouth and become quite a severe bit. The mouthpiece can be a straight bar or jointed. The straight bar will have a similar effect on the horse that the straight bar snaffle does but the jointed mouthpiece can become more severe as more pressure is focused on the bars and because of the curb action of the bit it can rotate forward and press into the tongue.

Below is a table showing the types of bits and mouthpieces and their effects on the horse.

Name of Bit	Affect on Horse
Loose ring snaffle 	A mild bit that can be used for training horses. The loose ring can pinch the lips so bit guards may be needed. It alerts the horse that the rider is about to engage the bit and so prepares the horse. It also encourages the horse to relax and chew the bit.

Egg butt snaffle	A mild bit which is more fixed in place in the mouth. Direct pressure is put on the tongue and bars in a nut cracker action.
D-ring	The bit rings are 'D' shaped. This prevents the mouthpiece from rotating and so secures it more in place. The shape of the rings can help the rider to direct the horse in lateral work.
Full cheeks	The cheeks prevent the bit from rotating and being pulled through the mouth. It also helps to guide the horse laterally. Bit keepers should be used with this bit.
Half cheeks	The cheeks help to prevent the bit being pulled through the horse's mouth like the full cheeked bit but it is less likely to get caught on anything and therefore is used more in racing.
Fulmer	A bit with full cheeks cannot rotate in the horse's mouth and it also prevents the bit from being pulled through the mouth. Keepers should be used to prevent the cheeks of the bit catching on anything. This bit can also help to guide the horse laterally.

Hanging cheek	The top rings of this bit allow the rider to exert pressure on the poll which causes the horse to round its neck.
Straight bar / mullen snaffle	A mild mouthpiece that applies even pressure on the tongue, bars and lips. It is usually made of hard rubber. The mullen is slightly raised in the centre to relieve tongue pressure. The straight bar does not do this.
Myler	The bit can twist in the mouth so the rider can put pressure on one side of the mouth to prevent both sides of the mouth feeling the bit move. This is meant to give the rider more precision.
Twisted mouthpiece	A severe bit that puts a lot of pressure on the horse's mouth. The pressure is increased because of the narrow parts of the twisted metal that come into contact with the horse's mouth.
French link	Most commonly used with a snaffle bit, the French link provides two joints which reduce the nut cracker action making the bit milder.
Double jointed snaffle	This has two joints which soften the nut cracker action as it follows the shape of the mouth better.

Snaffle with cherry roller	Nervous horses can benefit from the rollers on this bit as they can help to reduce nerves when the horse rolls their tongue over them. This can help the horse to relax and accept the bit. It also encourages salivation.
Cambridge snaffle	A straight bar bit with a raised semi-circle in the middle (known as a port) to relieve tongue pressure. The port is low so avoids poking the roof of the mouth. A very mild bit (depending on thickness).
Pelham	A curb bit that provides a leverage action as it puts pressure on the poll, bars, tongue and chin groove. This bit causes the horse to bring their head in towards their body. The mouthpiece can vary in type as can the rings and cheeks. Shanks can also vary in length which affects the severity of the curb action.
Rugby pelham	The rugby pelham has a loose ring which the snaffle rein attaches to. This gives the impression that the horse is wearing a double bridle. Some horses do not have room in their mouth for two bits so they cannot wear a double bridle which is sometimes preferred for showing.

Weymouth bit 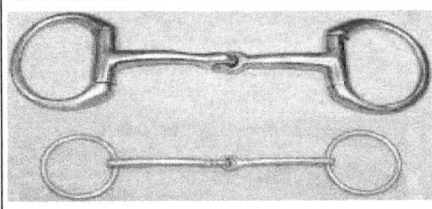	A curb bit that is used with a bradoon as part of a double bridle. Curb reins attach to the shanks of this bit. The mouth piece can vary – similar to the pelham.
Bradoon 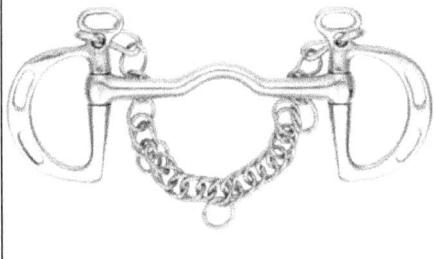	A snaffle bit that is used as part of a double bridle. The bit is smaller than a usual snaffle. A normal egg butt snaffle (top) is compared against a loose ring bradoon (bottom).
Kimblewick 	This bit has short shanks, D rings and a curb chain. It is classed as a curb bit though the curb action is very mild. Only one set of reins are used with this bit. Some kimblewicks have slots in the bit rings to thread the reins through so the bit can either be used as a snaffle bit (reins are threaded through top slots) or it can be used as a curb bit to create mild pressure on the poll (reins are threaded through bottom slots).
Curb chain	Applies pressure to the chin groove when the curb rein is used.

Lip strap	Helps to keep the curb chain flat and prevents loss if the chain comes off.
Curb chain cover or leather curb chain	Softens the pressure that the horse feels from the curb chain.
Liverpool bit	Used for driving horses, this bit allows the driver to attach the reins further down the shanks to get more curb action from a distance.
Cheltenham gag	The bit rings of this gag have a hole in the top and a hole in the bottom. A gag cheek piece (a length of rounded leather) is passed through these two holes. One end is attached to the head piece and the other end attaches to the reins. The gag is pulled up in the mouth and rotated slightly when activated. This particular bit is an egg butt and can be used as a snaffle if the reins are attached directly to the bit rings without the use of the sliding cheek pieces.

Dutch gag 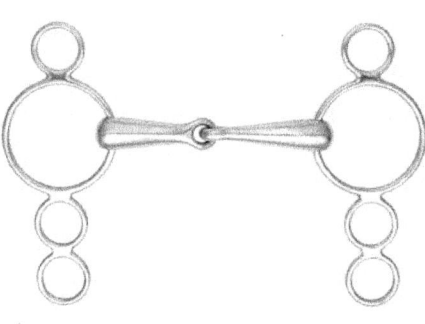	Two reins should be used with this bit. One set attaches to the bit rings and a second set attaches to one of the lower rings and should only be used when the horse is getting strong. The horse can be ridden normally with just the first set of reins. The second set cause the bit to be lifted in the mouth slightly and pressure is increased at the poll. The lower the hole used the more poll pressure is felt.
American gag 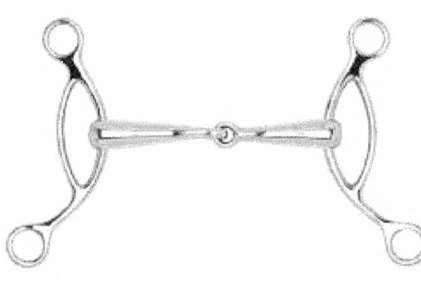	The mouthpiece of this gag is attached to sliding cheek pieces. These are what provide the leverage and cause the bit to raise in the mouth. Pressure is put on the poll and sides of the mouth. The bit can be used with one or two sets of reins. If two sets of reins are used the action of the bit is generally milder whereas one set of reins attached to the hole at the bottom of the shank increases the severity.
Chifney 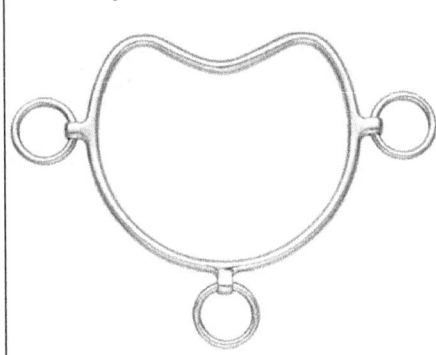	Also known as an anti-rearing bit, this bit helps the handler to lead the horse if they tend to get excited or rear up when being lead. They are particularly useful for turning out strong, excitable horses. If the horse tries to lift its head up or pull the handler then the mouthpiece will press into the tongue and the horse will slow down or bring their head down.

Bit Materials

As if it wasn't confusing enough having so many types of bits to choose from there is also quite a range of bit materials to choose from too. Some materials can alter the severity of a bit and others can have other interesting effects on the horse. These are listed below.

- Aurigan – 85% copper and free from nickel.

- Chrome plated – Looks good but poor quality because the chrome peels off.

- Copper – Encourages the production of saliva by oxidising in the mouth.

- German silver – Copper and nickel alloy. Gold in colour.

- Happy mouth – A white synthetic material. Softer on the horse's mouth but can get chewed up.

- Kangaroo – 70% copper and 30% nickel.

- Korsteel klasse – 88% copper alloy and free from nickel.

- Korsteel kröne – Made from brass, nickel and copper and is silver in colour.

- Nickel – A soft metal which tastes unpleasant. Some horses are allergic to this yellowish coloured metal.

- Nylon – Harder than the rubber bit and usually grey in colour.

- Stainless steel – Tastes pleasant and is the most common metal used to make bits.

- Sweet iron – A tasty bit for the horse which encourages the production of saliva. This bit will rust if it is not used regularly.

Competition Grooming

Clipping

Figure 96: The horse's thick winter coat is great for the colder weather but not ideal for showing or regular exercising.

Sometimes, especially in winter, the horse's coat gets a bit long and can start to look scruffy. Even though it is good for the horse to grow a thicker, longer coat **(Fig. 96)** to help them keep warmer when the weather gets harsher and colder it is difficult to make a coat like this look neat and tidy for showing. The horse will also get hot and sweaty quickly when they are worked and the tack can become uncomfortable for them too. If they are exercised a lot then it would be better to clip the coat. The horse is clipped according to their needs and the riders or owner's needs. There are various different ways to clip a horse – you do not have to clip the entire coat off.

Before clipping the horse you will need to get your tools and work area prepared. Your work area will need to be kept tidy for safety reasons so you will have to think about where you are going to put things so that they are accessible for you but out of the way and not within the horse's reach.

You will need:

- ⅄ Clippers **(Fig. 97)**

- ⅄ Clipper oil

- ⅄ Extension cable with circuit breakers

- ⅄ Grooming kit

- ⅄ A stick of white chalk (or a darker colour if the horse is grey)

- ⅄ PPE (Work boots and riding hat)

- ⅄ A rug for the horse

Figure 97: Horse clippers are similar to those used by a hair dresser only they are slightly bigger because they are heavy duty.

Start by preparing the clippers. You will need to make sure they are clean and not clogged up with hair. If they are you will need to take the head apart and clean it out. This is done by undoing the tension nut and the screws that hold the blade in place. Remove the blade and, using a little brush, brush off any hair. Brush any hair out from the clipper head where the blade is held in place then apply a small amount of clipper oil to this area and replace the blade, securing it in place with the screws and tension nut. Apply a small amount of clipper oil to the tip of the blade too.

Plug the clippers into an extension cord so you have plenty of room to get all around the horse without struggling. The extension cord must contain a circuit breaker so if there is an accident or the horse treads on the cord there is less risk of electrocution to yourself or the horse. Try to keep the cord off the floor and out of the path of the horse and never put the cord over the horse. You can get cordless clippers which are obviously safer but these can run out of power – not great if you are halfway through clipping a horse! If you are using cordless clippers try to make sure they are fully charged beforehand or have several fully charged batteries at the ready.

Once your clippers are ready fetch the horse and tie them up with a quick release knot. It would be a wise idea to wear work boots and a riding hat while clipping in case the horse spooks which is more common during clipping because of the noise and vibration of the clippers.

Give the horse a quick groom so there is no mud or dirt on the areas that are going to be clipped. Take a piece of chalk and draw an outline on the horse to show the areas that need clipping. Try to make sure that what you have drawn is level and is in exactly the right position on both sides of the horse. When you are ready to start clipping take the clippers and take a few steps away from the horse first and remain in the horse's sight. Turn the clippers on and watch how the horse reacts. When the horse seems settled with the noise of the clippers move slowly up to the horse and put the clippers (pointing upwards) against the area that needs clipping and move them downwards so that no hair is clipped. This allows the horse to get used to the feel of the vibration of the clippers before you get started. If the horse seems happy enough with you doing this you can then begin to clip.

Keep the blade flat against the horse's body **(Fig. 98)** and move the clippers into the hair. After each movement lift the clippers up and away from the horse to allow the loose hair to fall. Check the heat of the clippers and blade regularly as they can quickly become hot. This will become

Figure 98: Notice how the clippers are flat and moving into

uncomfortable for the horse so before they get too warm turn them off and allow them to cool. Add a few drops of clipper oil to the clippers every five to ten minutes to keep them working smoothly.

Take care when clipping near to the horse's head. The sound of the clippers will get louder for them as you get closer to their head so they may become jumpy or nervous. Keep an eye on the horse's body language. Talk to them and reassure them if they look unsettled. Horses that are head shy may not let you anywhere near their head with clippers so only clip this area if you really need to. Hold the horse's head with one hand to keep them still and clip with the other hand.

If the horse does not stand still or is nervous while you are clipping try distracting them or get someone to help you. Turning a radio on while using the clippers could help as this will help to drown out the sound.

When you think you have finished clipping give the horse a quick brush down with a soft body brush to remove any loose hair then take a step back and look over the areas you have clipped. Check that the clipped hair is all even and that you have not missed any patches. Check that the areas clipped on both sides of the horse are level and in line with each other. If you are not happy make your adjustments and look over the horse again. When you are happy with the clip put the rug on the horse and walk them around a bit to warm them up. It is important to keep a horse rugged up when they are clipped because they will now get cold easily. When you have put the horse away, unplug the clippers and clean the head out. Sweep all the hair up and put all tools and cables away tidily.

There is a wide range of clippers available now. If you are buying clippers look for ones that are quiet as noisy clippers can make a horse nervous and jumpy. Some are also easier to disassemble than others so look out for ones that allow you to remove the blade easily as you will need to do this a lot for maintenance.

Types Of Clip

Neck and belly clip

Suitable for horses in light work, the hair is cut off in the area where the horse sweats the most.

Low trace clip

Suitable for horses in light work and helps to prevent them from getting too sweaty.

High trace clip

Suitable for horses in light to medium work, more hair is clipped off to help the horse cool down due to the exercise being more strenuous.

Blanket clip

Suitable for horses who are worked regularly, this clip helps to keep the horse cool during exercise so they do not overheat.

Hunter clip

Suitable for horses who are regularly worked hard. The horse may need an exercise rug on to begin with so they do not get cold.

Full clip

Suitable for horses who are worked very hard and are used to compete at a high level. Care must be taken to make sure the horse is kept warm at all times, especially when stabled and turned out.

Trimming

Horses are trimmed in
several different places to
make them look tidier when
being prepared for a show.
The areas normally trimmed
are the legs, **(Fig. 99)** tail,
and head. Trimming these
areas neatens up the horse
and gives them a sharper
outline. Do make sure
beforehand though that the
horse you are trimming

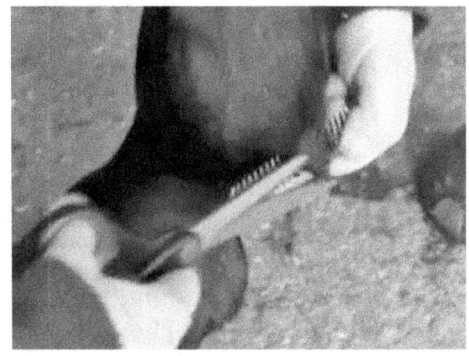

*Figure 99: Trimming the horse's
fetlocks.*

should actually be trimmed. This is because for some shows
certain breeds of horses are left to look natural. An example of
this is the native breeds. These are shown with a full length mane
and tail. If you are unsure then it is best to ring the show office
that you are planning on going to and ask beforehand.

If the horse is going to be living out then it would be advisable
not to trim the horse as these longer hairs protect them from the
elements.

The Tail

When trimming the tail you must first get all of the tangles out so
that the tail is even and falling naturally when trimmed. Brushing
the tail with a plastic curry comb or human hair brush may seem
easy but this will ruin the tail. Brushes pull at the hair and can
remove quite a lot, leaving the tail looking short, thin and wispy
at the bottom. This is because it takes a while for the hair to grow
back and it is not always a good look when showing. The judges
are more impressed when they are presented with a horse proudly
carrying a full, tidy tail. The best way to remove the tangles from
the tail is to take the whole tail in one hand then, a bit at a time,

release a small amount of hair and run your fingers through it with your other hand. Hair will still come out and it may take longer but less hair comes out this way.

When trimming the tail you should try to avoid making it so short that it goes above the horse's hocks. This is too short. Don't forget, the horse needs its tail to swat at flies! If you are trimming your own horse's tail then it is up to you how short you want it but it is recommended not to go above the hocks. The ideal length is in line with the horse's chestnuts. If you are trimming someone else's horse then you should always ask how much they want taken off beforehand. This is because if you go ahead and trim it and it is shorter than the owner would have liked they will be unhappy with it for some time as it takes a while for the tail to grow back. If they show the horse then you need to make sure that then length of the tail will not affect their chance to show. Trimming the tail of a native pony may particularly annoy their owner!

Figure 100: Grasp the hair and trim off below your hand.

Trimming the tail regularly or when needed will help to keep it neat, square and a suitable length.

To trim the horse's tail, after removing all of the tangles, you should take a hold of the tail at the top then run your hand down it and stop near the bottom. Hold the hair firmly then trim the hair off (**Fig. 100**) with your other hand using a pair of round ended scissors (these are safer as you cannot cause too much injury to the horse if you jab them by accident if they are fidgety). It is best to trim off the hair a bit at a time. You can always take more length off if the tail is still too long. If you cut the tail too short straight away there is no going back! Once you think you are finished, run your hand down the tail again and grip it at the bottom to make sure it all looks the same length and you have not missed any hairs. If it looks okay release the tail and take a few steps back. Looking at the tail from a distance you should be able to see if it is straight and even at the bottom. Job done.

Always remember to stand to the side of the horse when you are doing anything behind them to avoid getting kicked.

The Legs

The hair down the back of the horse's legs can be trimmed to give a neater outline of the leg. To do this you need to use round ended scissors and a comb – a mane comb or pulling comb should be fine. Use the comb to lift the hair up and away from the leg then trim along the surface of the comb. You should be trimming upwards so that all the hair is cut to the same length. Higher up the leg there may be some longer, thinner hairs that go right up the inside of the horse's leg and up to the point of

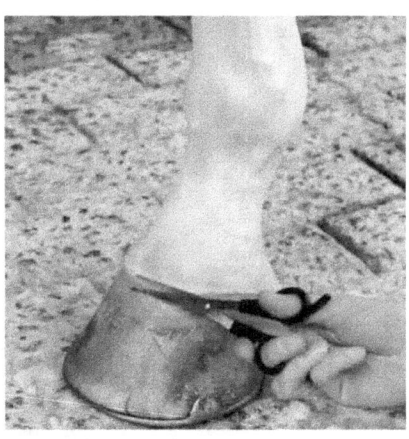

Figure 101: Trimming along the coronary band. Notice how the short hair on this horse's leg makes the leg appear more defined.

buttocks on the back legs. This can all be trimmed off too.

If the horse has feathers and you want to keep these you can tidy them up by trimming them so that the hair does not touch the floor but instead follows the shape of the foot. If the feathers are thin and uneven and you would rather remove them completely you can trim them off so the hair is the same length as that surrounding it **(Fig. 101)**. The feathers are also an area that should be allowed to grow naturally if they are being shown as a native breed so check beforehand if these should be trimmed or not.

The Head

Using round ended scissors trim off the longer hairs that appear over the cheeks (along the path of the bridle) and those that grow down from the horse's jaws **(Fig. 102)**. This makes the head look more defined. The whiskers around the horse's muzzle and the beard (if they have one) can also be trimmed, however, if the horse is living out then these whiskers should be left alone as they are sensitive and can help the horse feel their way around in the dark. This helps to reduce the risk of injuries and for this same reason the whiskers around the eyes should never be trimmed – whether the horse is stabled or living out.

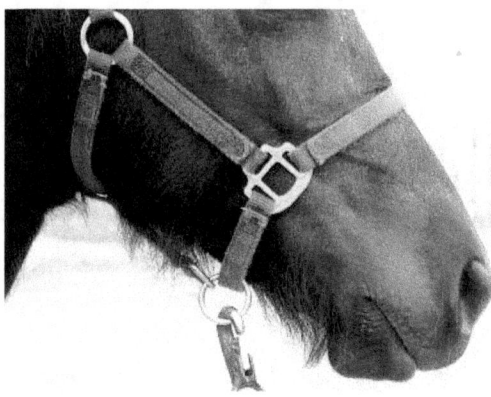

Figure 102: Notice the long hairs around the lower part of the horse's head. See how they make the head look fluffy rather than giving a crisp outline.

The ears can be trimmed if they are starting to look a bit woolly but be prepared in case the horse is not happy with this. If the horse is head shy and disapproves to having their ears touched you can try to distract them by putting a few treats in a bowl on the floor in front of them. Some chopped up apple or carrot should do the trick. This will help to take their mind off what you are doing, will keep their head still and it will bring them down to a lower level so you do not have to stretch and strain to reach those ears! Be gentle and quick while trimming the ears and reassure the horse with your voice. Have someone assist you if the horse is particularly troublesome.

Start by trimming any longer hairs off the outside of the ears with a pair of round ended scissors. Next, pinch the two edges of the ear together and trim off any hair that pokes out. Any hair inside the ear must be left alone. This hair is there to protect the inside of the horse's ear. Removing the hair can increase the horse's risk of developing ear infections or getting ear mites. It can also make the horse more sensitive around water as they dislike getting water in their ears.

The Mane

The mane should not really be trimmed as it takes on an unnatural, thick and boxy appearance **(Fig. 103)**. Longer hairs are usually pulled from the mane to gradually make it look naturally shorter. Some horses, however, will not stand for this so using scissors may be your only option. If this is the case begin by removing all tangles with a mane comb then trim the hair with some round ended scissors pointing upwards towards the horse's crest rather than horizontally. Trimming upwards can still look unnatural but it looks less boxy than cutting the hair straight across **(Fig.104)**.

Figure 103: *An example of how a poor trim can leave the mane looking boxy and uneven in length. This mane was trimmed with the scissors horizontal.*

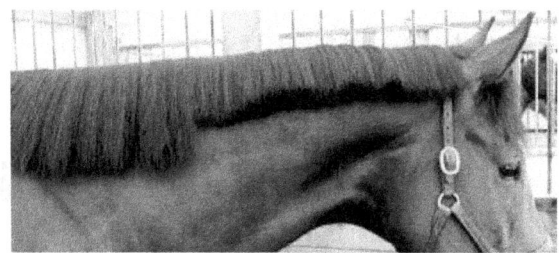

Figure 104: *A horse that has been trimmed properly with the scissors pointing upwards to make the mane appear neat and natural.*

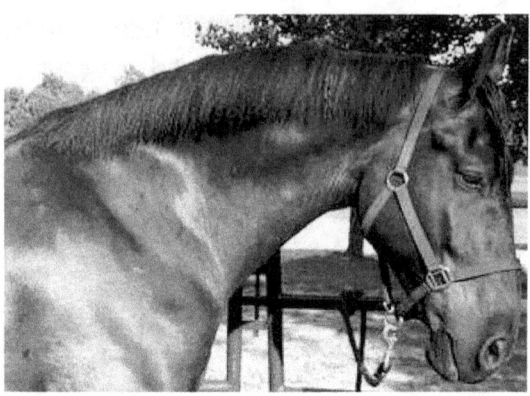

If there are any long hairs growing on or around the horse's withers now would be a good time to trim them. Be careful not to nip the horse with the scissors because of the shape of the horse's body here.

Figure 105: This mane has been pulled and is a nice even length all the way along.

If the forelock needs trimming this can be cut straight across because the hair here is usually thinner and will not look to unnatural if cut in this way. If the forelock is particularly thick you can cut upwards as with the mane if you want to avoid the 'massive square fringe' look. When trimming the forelock, or anywhere around the horse's head, be very aware of the horse's movements – getting poked in the eye with scissors is not very pleasant and a sharp, unexpected jab can startle the horse causing them to panic.

Pulling

Pulling the mane and tail help to keep them looking tidy. Hairs are pulled out to tidy up the top of the tail and to shorten the mane so it looks naturally shorter **(Fig. 105 – 108)** rather than trimmed. It is best to pull on a hot day or just after

Figure 106: Notice how this pulled mane looks natural at the ends and is not square or angled in any way.

exercise as the heat causes the horse's pores to open so the hairs come out easier.

To pull the mane you will need a narrow pulling comb. First, comb the mane to remove any tangles then take a hold of a few longer hairs at the bottom. Comb upwards to push the shorter hairs up out of the way then wrap the longer hairs around the comb and in one quick tug pull the comb down to remove the hairs. It is better to try and do this quickly and confidently as hesitating or slow pulling can be more uncomfortable for the horse. Always start with the longer hairs as this way you will be able to gradually shorten the mane to the preferred length. You should aim to have the mane straight and the same length along the whole of the neck if possible. Try not to spend too long working on the hairs at the poll as this area is more sensitive and the horse may begin to fidget and get moody. Starting lower down the neck and working your way up to the poll may help to desensitise the horse, making it less uncomfortable for them at the poll. This is because the horse's body begins to produce endorphins. These endorphins will reduce the amount of pain the horse feels – making it less uncomfortable for them when you get to the poll. The forelock may also be pulled to shorten it though if the horse will not allow you to do this it can be trimmed instead.

Pulling the tail is not something that can be done on all horses. This is because the horse can quite easily kick out and the situation can become too dangerous. It is too risky just to achieve a neater tail. If the horse is happy with this being done then just remember to always stand to the side of the horse when working behind them. If you are unsure how the horse is going to react then you can try giving the horse a haynet to help distract them or even try pulling their tail over their stable door or put a hay bale behind them – this way you cannot get kicked but you can see if the horse will actually disapprove and kick out. As this task can be dangerous it would be a wise idea to wear PPE (Personal Protective Equipment) while doing this. Work boots, a hat and a body protector will help in case there are any accidents.

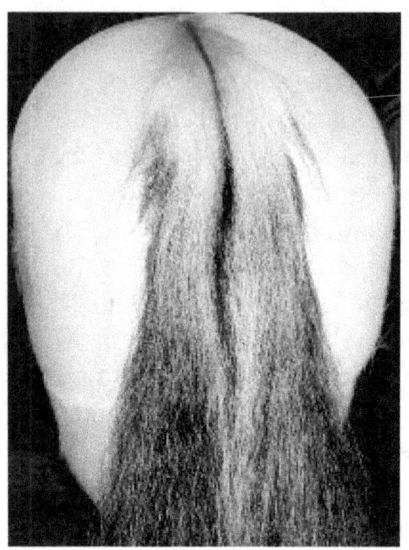 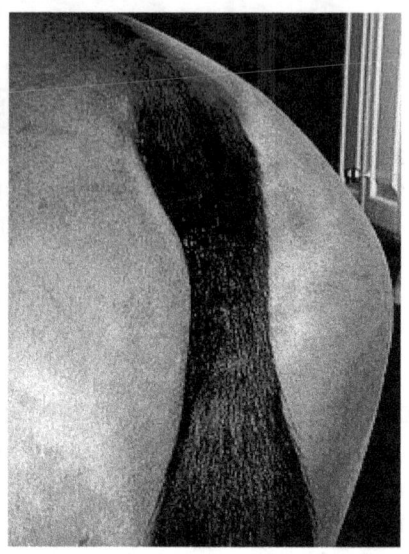

Figure 107: A full tail which has not been pulled. This tail would be good for plaiting.

Figure 108: A pulled tail which shows off the shape of the horse. This tail would be difficult to plait.

To pull the tail make sure the horse has had a good exercise beforehand so their pores are nice and open. Also, make sure the tail and dock area are clean and the tail is tangle free. You will need a pulling comb and some plasters to remove the hairs. The hairs that should be removed are at the sides and underneath on the top third of the tail. The short hairs will be too short to pull with the pulling comb so you will need to pull these out with your fingers. This is what the plasters are for! If you can, wrap the shorter hairs around your finger then pull down quickly and firmly to remove the hairs. If you do this without plasters on your finger it will soon get sore. If it is difficult to get a grip on the short hairs try wearing a pair of surgical rubber gloves. These make it easier to grip the hair. The longer hairs can be pulled out with the pulling comb. Like with the mane, take hold of a few hairs and comb the rest upwards out of the way then wrap the longer hairs around the comb a few times and firmly pull down to remove them. Talk to the horse and reassure them to help keep them calm.

Plaiting

When the mane and tail are tidy and an even length it makes plaiting up much easier. The plaits in the mane will be shorter making it quicker to plait up and the tail will be tidier making the plait look neater and straighter.

There are many ways to plait a mane, the most common being rolled up plaits. There are two ways to secure these rolled up plaits and the first and easiest way is to use small elastic bands. Another way is to use a needle and thread. This can take a bit longer but with practice it is easy enough and the plait is held a lot more firmly in place. To do this you need:

- A large, blunt ended needle

- Cotton that matches the colour of the mane

- A small bucket of water

- Water brush

- Mane comb

- Small elastic bands

- Sturdy stool

- Scissors

You will need to prepare your needle and thread before each plait so it is ready when you need it. Cut a piece of cotton to approximately the length of your arm. Thread the cotton through the needle and knot the two ends together so the cotton is double thickness. This makes the thread stronger. If you want to avoid having to prepare the needle before each plait then use several needles and prepare them all at the same time using a shorter length of cotton. Make sure you put these somewhere safe – an apron with a pocket is great. You can have your needles, cotton, scissors and bands at hand when you need them.

Begin by leading the horse to your work area and tying them up with a quick release knot. If you are preparing the horse for a show give the horse a thorough groom as described earlier. If you are just plaiting the mane to get the hair out of the way or even just for practice then you can get straight to it. Stand on the stool so you do not have to reach up to get to the mane or else before you know it your arms will be aching! Make sure the mane has had a good brush through then separate the hair into an odd number of bunches (each bunch should be about as wide as a mane comb) and hold each one in place with an elastic band. Remove the band from your first bunch at the top and dampen the hair with a wet water brush. This keeps the hair together and makes the plait look neater. Alternatively you can use egg white in the same way. This acts like a gel and holds the hair together more firmly. Plait the hair as far down as you can nice and tightly. This reduces the risk of it looking messy and coming loose. When you get to the bottom take the needle and cotton and thread it through the end of the plait, sew through it a couple of times and wrap it around the end twice to hold all of the hair together. Fold the wispy end under, wrap the cotton around it a few times then sew through it again to hold it in place. Fold the plait in half so the end of the plait is now underneath the top of the plait and thread the needle through the top of the plait from underneath so the top and bottom of the plait are secured together. Sew down the plait so the two halves are held together. When you get to the bottom fold the plait underneath again and sew in place as you did for the first fold. Finally, thread the needle through from underneath at the top and wrap the cotton around to the right of the plait and thread the needle back through the underneath of the plait. Now wrap the cotton around to the left and thread the needle back through the bottom of the plait. Thread the needle through the nearest stitch and back through the loop you have just created then pull it tight. Thread the needle through the balled up plait and cut off the remaining cotton close to the plait.

If you are plaiting up the horse in the stable with a needle and thread sweep the bedding back first. This gives you a better chance of finding the needle if you drop it!

The number of plaits you would put down the horse's neck can vary depending on how long or short the horse's neck is. If the horse has a long neck then putting fewer plaits in will help make the neck look in proportion to the body. In the same way more plaits along a short neck will give the appearance of a longer neck. Either way you should aim for an odd number of plaits along the neck so when the forelock is plaited you have an even number of plaits.

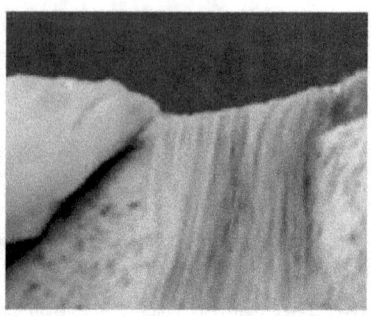

Step 1: Separate the mane into bunches the width of a mane comb or roughly four fingers.

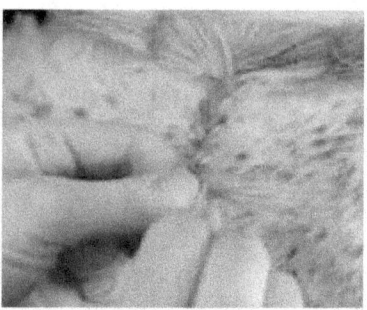

Step 2: Starting from the top bunch, plait down the hair as far as you can, keeping the plait tight.

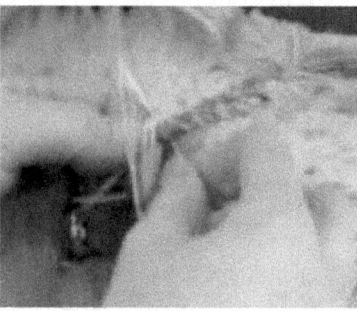

Step 3: Sew through the end of the plait then fold the wispy end under and wrap the thread around it a few times. Sew through it again for a neat end.

Step 4: Thread the needle through the top of the plait from underneath.

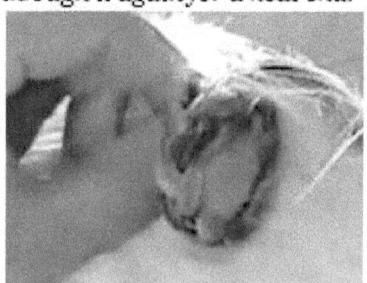

Step 5: Pull the thread to bring the bottom of the plait up to meet the top of the plait then sew down the plait to hold the two halves together.

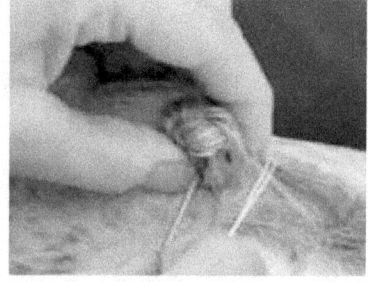

Step 6: Fold the plait in half. Put the needle through the base of the plait and bring the needle around to the right and back through the base. Repeat this to the left of the plait.

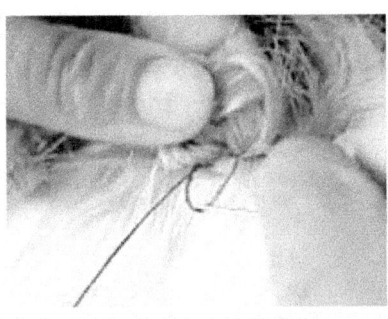

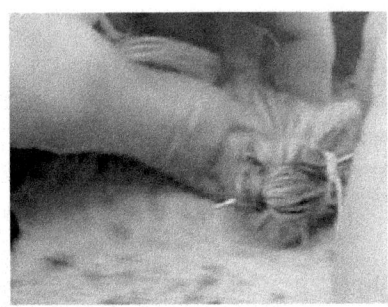

Step 7: Thread the needle through a nearby stitch and put the needle through the loop you have just created. Pull the thread to create a knot and repeat a couple of times in the same place.

Step 8: Thread the needle through the centre of the plait so the thread comes out near the underneath.

Step 9: Cut off the thread where it exits the plait.

Plaiting the tail is a bit like an accessory – nice but not necessarily needed. If the horse will not allow you to pull their tail then plaiting is a good way to make the tail look neater for a show because you can include all of the shorter hair at the edges into the plait. The tail can still be plaited even if it has been pulled. The plait will look straighter and tidier.

A French plait is what is usually put in the tail. This can take a bit of practice if you have not done one before but once you have the knack it will come naturally. As with the mane, the plait in the tail can be secured either with elastic bands or with a needle and thread. The process is similar to plaiting the mane and you will need all of the same equipment apart from the stool.

Begin by preparing your work area and threading your needle with cotton that matches the colour of the horse's tail. Fetch the horse and tie them up using a quick release knot. To plait the tail make sure it is clean first and remove all of the tangles with your fingers. Remember to stand to the side of the horse. If you have to wash the tail first then avoid using any type of conditioner as this will make the hair slippery and difficult to plait. Dampen the top of the tail down to the bottom of the tail bone so the hair is easier to work with. Starting right at the top of the tail, take a small amount of hair from the left and right sides and the same amount from the hair in between. Begin the plait by crossing over the left and right pieces as you would a normal plait but then as you go to cross them over the next time add another piece of hair to the existing strand. The hair you take should be from right around the side of the tail. Continue to do this on both sides every time you cross hair over. When the French plait has reached the end of the tail bone you can stop adding hair from the sides and continue to plait the remaining hair that you have collected. Plait right down to the bottom then you can either secure the end with an elastic band or you can sew through the end as you would when plaiting the mane. When the end is secure fold the plait underneath to where the French plait ends **(Fig 109)**. If you are using elastic bands then secure the plait in place here with a band. If you are using a needle and thread put the needle through the plait at the base of the French plait from underneath. Pull the cotton through and wrap it around to the right and thread the needle up through the plait again from underneath. Do the same again but this time to the left. Repeat this 3 – 4 times until the plait feels secure then thread the needle through the nearest stitch and thread the needle through the loop you have just created. Thread the needle back through the plait so the cotton comes out at the back of the tail then cut it off close to the plait.

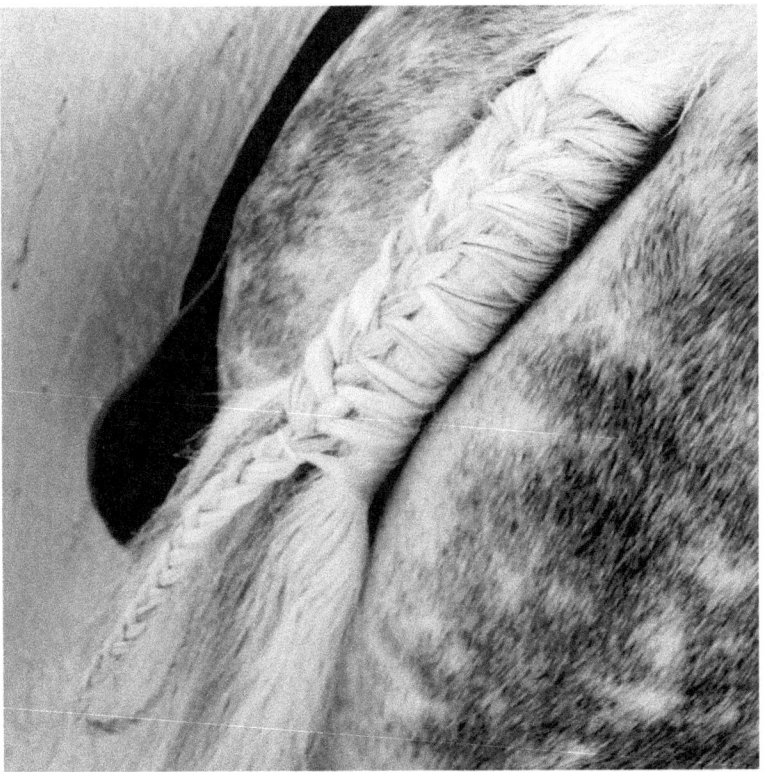

Figure 109: A tail plaited in the style of a French plait then folded under and secured with an elastic band.

Bathing Methods

There are a few ways of getting the horse clean for a show rather than just giving them a bath from head to toe. This is not always necessary. You can wash down the area that is dirty, give a partial bath or even just hot towelling can make a horse look spick and span. If the horse has a couple of patches of dirt on them then washing these off with warm water and shampoo should do the trick and the horse will look ready to be groomed and plaited up for the show. Just make sure you get the horse nice and dry first or else you may have a curly-haired horse on your hands!

Partial Bathing

A partial bath involves washing the mane, tail and socks. The horse can be kept rugged up for this. Before washing the mane undo the surcingles on the horse's rug then knot them together so they do not dangle down. If the rug has leg straps uncross these and fasten them to the loop on the same side without putting the strap around the leg. Undo the straps at the horse's chest then fold the rug back on itself to avoid getting the rug wet. Wet the mane with warm water and a sponge then lather it up with shampoo. Rinse thoroughly with clean warm water then dry as best as you can with towels. Once you have dried

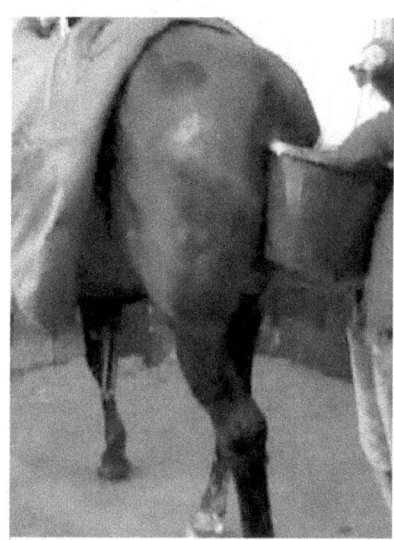

Figure 110: Washing the horse's tail. Notice how the rug is folded well out of the way.

the mane as much as possible fold the rug forwards into its normal position but leave the chest straps undone. This is because the horse's tail and socks still need to be washed and if the horse were to bolt the rug could slip around and become a hazard for the horse if it is still done up somewhere.

To wash the horse's tail the rug will need to be out of the way so, making sure all straps are unfastened, fold the rug back onto the hind quarters so the tail is completely revealed. Dip the horse's tail in a bucket of clean, warm water and lift the bucket up as high as you can to submerge as much tail as possible **(Fig. 110)**. Sponge water over the top of the tail so all of the hair is wet. Shampoo the whole tail and really work it into the dock area to remove all of the scurf and dirt. Rinse by submerging the tail in the bucket of water again to remove the majority of the foam. It may take a while to rinse so use the sponge to rinse the top of the tail then pour clean water over the tail to wash out any residue. When this is done, wring out and spin the tail. You can now fold the rug back down and fasten it up.

Washing the horse's socks is much easier as the rug is not in the way so just wet the area with a wet sponge, lather up with shampoo then rinse thoroughly with the sponge. Dry the legs off with a towel afterwards.

Hot Towelling

The hot towelling method is used if the horse is clipped but needs cleaning, if the horse is perhaps a bit dusty but not in need of a bath or if it is winter and it is too cold to bath. This method of cleaning removes sweat and grease from the horse's body and leaves them with a shiny coat.

To hot towel a horse you will need the following:

- ⅄ One bucket of very hot water (as hot as you can handle)

- ⅄ A small amount of shampoo (about one tea spoon to go into the water)

- ⅄ One small towel or several flannels

- ⅄ Two to three large, dry towels

If the horse is wearing a rug you will have to undo and fold the rug back to get to the areas that need cleaning like for a partial bath. Start by putting the small towel or flannel in the bucket of water then wring it out really well. Start at the horse's head and rub the towel all over the forelock, ears and face. Dip and wring the towel every time it becomes cool. Proceed down the mane, neck, body, tail then legs.

Dry the horse off with the large, dry towels or put the horse in a solarium if this is available to you. Make sure the horse is kept warm by rugging them up or walking them around. If you are hot towelling the horse while they are rugged up then make sure you dry the wet areas off before folding the rug back over it. You may need another clean, dry rug for when you have finished as the rug the horse is wearing may become damp if their coat is still a bit wet when the rug is placed back.

Methods of Restraint

If the horse refuses to stand still or is too nervous to be bathed safely there are some things you can do to make it easier. Always try to distract the horse first then if this does not work you can try methods of restraint.

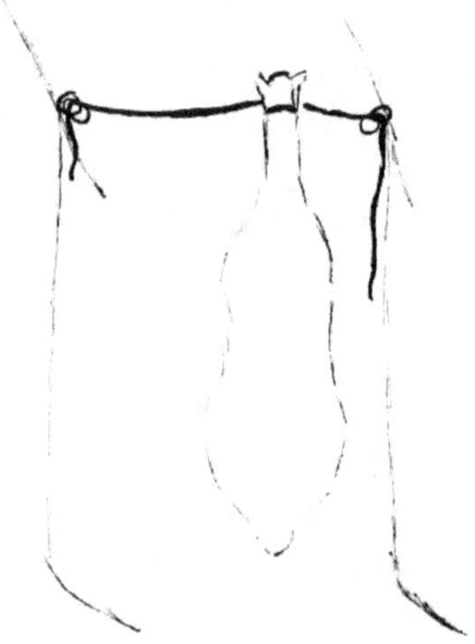

If you are trying to trim one of the horse's legs and they keep lifting their leg up get someone to come and lift up and hold their other leg on the same side. So if you are trying to trim the left rear leg but the horse keeps lifting it up or is kicking out – get someone to hold up the left front leg. Now the horse cannot lift the hind leg and you can get the job done. This is also useful with a fidgety horse.

Figure 111: A horse tied to two poles to help keep its front end still. The length of the ropes can be altered to allow you room to work down the one side of the horse if they are in a stall such as the one in this drawing.

If you need the horse to keep its head still then something as simple as getting someone to come and hold the horse for you can make all the difference. Your helper can help to hold the horse's head still, sooth them and even feed them a few pieces of carrot to help keep the horse occupied while you do what needs to be done. Your helper should always stand on the same side of the horse as you. This is because if the horse spooks at what you are doing they are going to jump away from you. If someone is standing on the other side of the horse they are going to get jumped on!

If no one is available to help you try attaching two lead ropes to the horse's head collar. Tie one lead rope to something solid to the left of the horse and tie the other lead rope to something solid to the right side of the horse **(Fig. 111)**.

Figure 112: A rope twitch.

If the horse is nervous or too active to the point where it is not safe to be working on them you can ask someone to come and put a twitch on the horse so that you can get on with the job in safety. A twitch is a device that is put around the horse's muzzle and tightened up. This causes the horse's body to release endorphins and the horse relaxes. It is their version of a natural high!

There are two versions of the twitch. There is the original twitch **(Fig. 112)** which is a pole with a loop of rope at the end and there is a clamp that is known as the humane twitch **(Fig. 113)**. This one is friendlier as it does not pinch the horse's muzzle whereas the rope can do this. Look out for the horse's body language to tell you they are relaxed. Their head and neck should droop down so their back and neck are in-line or thereabouts. Their eyes should look almost sleepy – not lively and darting around. Their ears should be slightly back and down (not in an aggressive manner though!). These signs should be visible after three to five minutes as this is how long it takes for the endorphins to be released. Once the twitch is on you should avoid touching the horse's muzzle as it becomes extremely sensitive. It would be very unpleasant for the horse and could cause them to react in a way that could compromise your safety. Try not to leave the twitch on for more than 15 minutes. This is because the effects of the twitch will begin to wear off and it is better to remove the

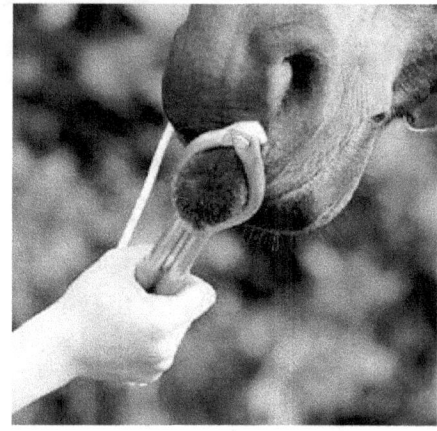

twitch while the horse is still experiencing the pleasant

Figure 113: A humane twitch.

effects of the twitch so they have good memories of this method and allow you to do it again in the future.

If the horse refuses to have the twitch you may have to call a vet out to sedate the horse **(Fig. 114)**. This method is very effective and you can get on with the tasks you need to do in safety. Do not ever let your guard down though. Continue to read the horse's body language and avoid doing things such as standing directly behind the horse. You will need to think about if it is really

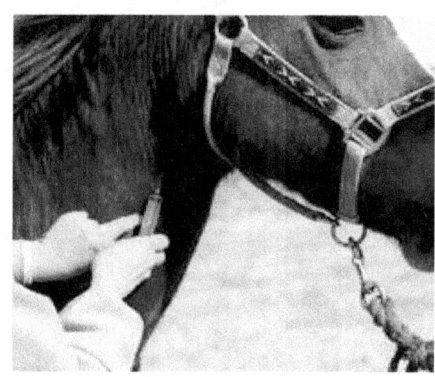

Figure 114: A horse being injected with sedative.

necessary for you to do whatever it is you are trying to do. Is it really worth putting the horse through this and is it worth the cost of a vet fee just to tidy them up a bit? It depends really on the importance of what it is you are trying to do and how often it would need to be done. This option is really something that should be thought about by weighing up the pros and cons.

Whenever you need to restrain a horse it is always best to use as little force and restraint as possible as this is more comfortable and safer for the horse and handler. Restraining the horse when it is not really needed could cause the horse to become nervous or head shy.

Transportation

Legal Requirements

There are a few things to take into account and check before loading horses into a lorry or trailer and driving off. For a start, the driver must be allowed to drive or tow a horse trailer or lorry. If the driver passed their driving test on or after January 1st 1997 they will be more restricted and will more than likely have to take a test to allow them to tow a trailer or drive a horse box or lorry. If the driver passed their test prior to this date they should check their drivers license to make sure they are allowed to drive a HGV or tow a trailer. Getting this wrong means you could void your insurance and you become an uninsured driver.

Once you are sure the driver is allowed by law to drive or tow you should make sure the vehicles are legal to go on the road. The lorry, horse box or towing vehicle should be taxed and in date until after you have finished using it. The tax disc should be visible on the left hand side of the wind screen at all times. A towing vehicle should have a valid MOT that should not run out before returning home. This means your vehicle is deemed fit for road use.

A lorry or horse box will also need a type of MOT known as plating. This is a bit like an MOT but more intensive to make sure the vehicle is fit for road use and safe for other road users. Plating needs to be carried out at a proper testing centre and the certificate should be kept up to date and be visible somewhere in the lorry. A valid MOT is also needed.

As with any vehicle that goes on the road, the lorry or towing vehicle should be insured with at least third party cover. This covers the cost of injury to other road users if you are involved in an accident. However, third party, fire and theft cover is advisable because these vehicles are not cheap and can get stolen. If your vehicle is stolen or catches fire and you are only insured third party you cannot claim a penny.

It is advisable to have your towing vehicle or lorry serviced annually or after a certain amount of miles to keep it in good working order. This helps to prevent unwanted breakdowns and sudden, unforeseen bills. It is not a legal requirement to have your vehicle serviced but it is a good idea to get it done at regular intervals to avoid getting stuck on the side of the road somewhere. This can become unpleasant for the horses and difficult for their handlers. Accidents could even be the result of something going wrong which could have been preventable had the vehicle been serviced.

Trailers should also be serviced regularly to keep them safe inside and out. It is imperative that they are working correctly for road use and also that they are safe and structurally sound inside for the sake of the horse. Serious accidents can happen when the holding areas are not cared for properly.

Weight Limits

When towing a trailer it is important to make sure you are abiding by the weight limit rules. The weight of the empty trailer plus the weight of the horse(s) should be below or equal to the maximum authorised mass (MAM) of the trailer. The combined weight of the horse(s) and trailer should be below or equal to the towing vehicles maximum towing capacity (MTC). You then need to make sure that the driver is still legal to drive the vehicle with the horse and trailer according to their driver's license as different weights can effect this.

Figure 115: This sign means the road ahead has a vehicle weight limit of 7.5 tonnes.

Horse boxes and lorries will also have a maximum authorised mass which should not be exceeded. This will include all horses that are loaded and any tack or other equipment stored in the horse box or lorry. Again, make sure that the weight of the load does not exceed the driver's legal limit.

Roads themselves can sometimes have weight limits **(Fig. 115)** so be sure you know the total weight of your vehicle and trailer (if used) before travelling down one of these roads. The weight limit will be displayed on a road sign usually before the entrance to the road. A weight limit is normally in place due to weak bridges or road conditions (usually narrow lanes) which is why it is important to plan your journey well in plenty of time.

Tachographs

If your horse box or trailer and towing vehicle weigh over 3.5 tonnes it is likely you will need to use a tachograph **(Fig. 116)**. This is a recording device that logs details of driving activity such as speed, hours of travel, length of breaks etc. They are used mainly in commercial vehicles (in this case

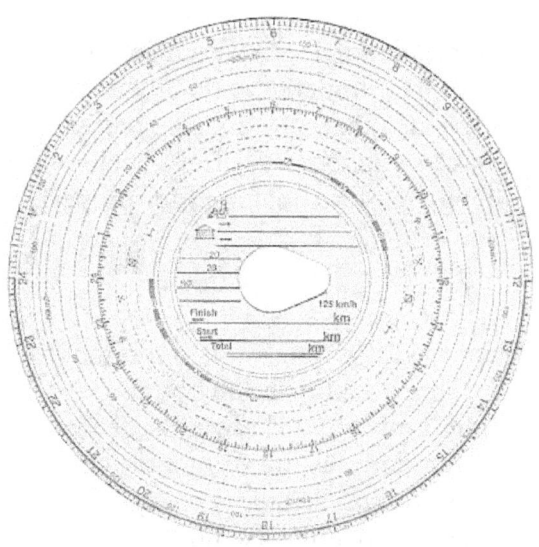

Figure 116: An example of a blank tachograph.

transporting horses for a financial reward) and are a legal requirement. They are used mainly to make sure that the driver does not exceed the maximum amount of hours they are allowed to drive and that they take breaks that are no shorter than the minimum set length. They are also used if the vehicle has been involved in an accident as they provide information that can help to clarify the cause of the incident.

A tachograph will only need to be used for private use if the vehicle is over 7.5 tonnes.

Whether for commercial or private use, the tachograph must be inspected every 2 years at a Department for Transport approved tachograph calibration centre. The tachograph should be recalibrated here every 6 years.

Safe Driving

Driving a car is one thing but driving while towing a horse trailer or driving a horse box is completely different. Your rear view becomes impaired, your combined weight is heavier which effects acceleration and braking, you take up more space on the road, it can be harder to manoeuvre and you must consider how your driving could affect the horses you are transporting.

The speed that you travel can greatly affect your horse's balance so whenever you need to change speed it should be done gradually and smoothly. Pulling away should be done slowly and in a straight line. This is to help the horse steady themselves and get used to the movement. When stopping, slowing, turning or approaching roundabouts you should begin to slow down in plenty of time. If you are going around a bend, turn or roundabout this should be done in a steady manner without alternating your speed. Only speed up when the vehicle is straight again or else all of the horse's weight could get shifted to one side causing them to lose their balance.

A safe and steady speed to travel at on main roads is 40-45mph (unless signs state otherwise). The speed limit for a horse box on a main road with a national speed limit is 50mph. When driving down lanes you should reduce your speed to around 30mph (again, unless stated otherwise). To play it safe it is best to travel below the speed limit as the limit is in place for normal vehicles.

You need to allow more time to slow when transporting horses so it is better to travel below the speed limit to compensate.

It is best to avoid narrow, twisty lanes on your route as these can be more dangerous for larger vehicles and you may need to brake suddenly. This along with constant shifting of body weight due to the bends can make for a miserable and uncomfortable journey for a horse. For the same reasons you should also try to avoid driving through town centres or down roads with lots of roundabouts as there can be lots of stopping and starting. Rush hour would be a good time to avoid travelling or take a break during this time if you are already on the road. This is because traffic can get heavy and the roads can become more dangerous when they are busier. Busy roads can also lead to lots of stopping and starting so rush hour is not an ideal time to transport horses.

Travelling on roads such as dual carriageways and motorways makes the journey safer and more comfortable for the horse. This is because there is more room on the roads for larger vehicles and there is a fast lane for other traffic to get past should they need to rather than overtaking into oncoming traffic. These types of roads are great for long journeys because you can cover large distances quickly and if there is an emergency of some kind and you need to pull over there is usually a hard shoulder. Do bare in mind that even though you may have pulled into a hard shoulder it is still a dangerous place to be so do not unload the horse(s), instead, leave them in the trailer or lorry and exit the vehicle to the left and wait on the verge for help.

Finally, always signal early to let other road users know your intentions and be courteous to other drivers who stop for you or give way.

Loading / Unloading Horses

Horses should only be loaded into a trailer or horse box after the holding area has been prepared and the horse is wearing protective travel clothing. The trailer or horse box ramp should be down and the partitions should be opened and fastened back (for a horse box or lorry) or the rear bar should be down (for a trailer). If there are gates for the sides of the ramp this is the time to securely put them in place. If you have not loaded a horse before it may be worth practising with a horse that loads easily to get the hang of how to do it correctly.

Before leading the horse to the trailer or horse box, make sure you are wearing adequate PPE so you are safe during the loading process. It is important to remember to keep yourself safe, not just the horse, because some horses can become difficult to handle during loading which can put the handler at risk. You should be wearing a riding hat, gloves with good grip and sturdy boots (preferably steel toe caps).

Ideally, you should have someone helping you as this makes the loading process safer. They too should also be wearing PPE.

Load the horse as follows:

1. Lead the horse in a straight line towards the centre of the ramp. Do not speed up or slow down on approach. Walk confidently and do not look at the horse.

2. Walk straight up the ramp at the same speed and lead the horse straight to the securing ring.

3. Trailer: Ask your helper to put the rear bar up then put the ramp up. You can then tie the horse to the string attached to the securing ring with a quick release knot. Exit through the jockey door, closing it securely behind you.

4. <u>Horse box / lorry:</u> Ask your helper to close the partition around the horse while you tie the horse to the string attached to the securing ring with a quick release knot. Exit the horse box / lorry and put the ramp up.

The ramp can be heavy to lift up and secure in place. If it is too heavy then seek help rather than struggling by yourself. Most trailer ramps can be put up by one person. When doing this you should first put any gates back up and secure them then stand in front of the ramp in the centre and lift it with bent knees and a straight back. Before the end of the ramp becomes too high put your hands flat on the surface of the ramp and walk your hands up it to continue closing the ramp. Once the ramp is up secure it in place on both sides. If the ramp you are putting up is for a horse box or lorry, ask for help. Stand to the side of the ramp and have the other person stand at the other side. Count to three and lift the ramp together in the same way as described for lifting a trailer ramp. Be sure to stand to the side of the ramp as much as possible rather than directly underneath it as these ramps are heavy and can cause serious injuries if they come down on someone.

If only one horse is being transported and the horse has to stand facing forwards rather than sideways load them into the right hand side of the trailer or horse box. The weight of the horse on the right hand side helps to balance the transportation. This is because of the camber on the road so the trailer or horse box would be inclined to lean to the left a bit. If the horse has been loaded into the left hand side of the transport there will be more weight on the left hand side which can cause balance issues and could even cause the transport to topple over if a corner is taken too fast.

Unloading the horse is basically like loading the horse – only in reverse! Be ready with your PPE and your helper.

Unload the horse as follows:

1. Untie the horse and take a firm hold of the lead rope then ask your helper to unfasten the ramp and lower it (if you are using a trailer with an additional ramp to the front then lower this one). They should also secure any gates in place down the sides of the ramp.

2. Ask your helper to let down the front bar (for a forward exiting trailer) or the rear bar (for a rear exiting trailer). If the horse is in a horse box or lorry ask your helper to unfasten and pull back the partition.

3. Lead the horse down the centre of the ramp steadily and slowly when your helper is standing to the side and out of the way. Horses in a rear exiting trailer should be backed down the ramp slowly and should not be turned around until they are off the ramp. Ask your helper to help keep the horse straight while backing them down the ramp to prevent the horse slipping off the edge.

4. Remove the horse's travel clothing then put the horse(s) away or turn them out.

5. Thoroughly clean the holding area of the trailer or horse box, not forgetting to clean the ramp.

6. Put the ramp up and lock the vehicle.

Sometimes it does not always go to plan and a horse may be difficult to load. At times it could just be that you did not approach the ramp in a confident, energetic way or in a straight line and this gives the horse an opportunity to dig their heels in. In this case, walk the horse around in a big circle and make the horse walk on with an energetic walk. Make sure to walk the horse in a straight line towards the centre of the ramp. Do not hesitate, look at the horse or change your speed. If the horse does not follow you up the ramp this time turn the horse in a big circle again and approach as before but this time with some treats in your left hand. Hold these out in front of you as you get to the ramp to encourage the horse to move towards the treats. If the horse steps onto the ramp with a good amount of energy let them get to the top of the ramp and over to their securing ring before giving them the treat. Tie them up then give them lots of praise. If the horse stops halfway up the ramp hold some more treats out in front of you and out of the horse's reach to encourage them to walk forwards. Tell them to walk on and avoid looking at them. If the horse still refuses to budge you will need some help. Your helper could try standing to the side of the horse's hind quarters with a whip and tap the horse with it to encourage them to move forwards. You could also try moving the partition out of the way (in the trailer) and bringing down the front ramp to make it look brighter and more inviting. If you know beforehand that the horse might be difficult to load you could try loading another horse first which can encourage the difficult loader to go and join them. You could also park the lorry or trailer alongside a wall as this can offer the horse a feeling of stability and security. If the horse is still unwilling to load you will need some help from a couple of people. Attach a lunge line to both sides of the lorry or trailer. One helper should stand either side of the ramp holding the lunge line. They should then cross to the opposite side while still holding the line so the two lines cross behind the horse. If the horse has not moved forward by this point the helpers should begin to pull the lines taut so that they start to put light pressure on the back of the horse's legs just above the hocks. If the horse wilfully begins to walk up the ramp take the pressure off the hind legs and let them continue while offering plenty of praise to the horse. If, however, the horse decides to stay put gradually increase the pressure on the legs until the horse does move forwards. Only remove the pressure when you are confident the horse will keep walking. This method can also be used if you have no one around to help you. Tie one lunge line to the right hand side of the lorry or trailer and bring the line around the rear of the horse while leading the horse with your left hand (standing to the left side of the horse). Gradually increase the pressure of the lunge line on the horse's legs to encourage them to walk on.

Always make sure that neither you nor your assistants stand right behind the horse. Try to read the horse's body language to see if they are scared or annoyed and adjust your method of handling the horse accordingly. Anyone assisting with loading the horse(s) should be wearing adequate PPE because loading horses can be a dangerous task – even with horses who normally load well. Team work is a must when it comes to loading as it makes the job easier and smoother. If you must load on your own try to get some practice at loading with help beforehand in case you find yourself in a situation where you are on your own and realise you need help.

Competing

When to Compete

The best time to compete your horse is when they are fit and are being schooled regularly. This way they have the agility and discipline to do what you are asking of them so they have a better chance of reaching their potential and doing well at the show. The horse will also need to be healthy and sound. Health issues can hamper the horse's ability to perform to their full potential and depending on the issue they may not even be allowed to compete. If the horse is not sound on the day chronic or acute lameness can ruin the horse's chances of competing.

Figure 117: This lady is doing piaffe on her horse - something that can only be done nicely if both she and her horse are well practised and working well together.

Competing is not all down to the preparation of the horse – the rider needs to be ready too! The rider also needs to be fit and healthy so they have the energy to instruct and control the horse during the competition. The rider should have had plenty of time to prepare for the show so they know their course or test and they should have had plenty of riding time so they are capable of competing well in the class they are entering.

When the horse and rider are working well together **(Fig. 117)** and the rider is confident the horse is listening to them and doing what is being asked of them – that is when to compete.

When Not to Compete

There are several factors that can affect the horse's way of going and the horse's overall health if they are competed at the wrong time. Some people think that if their horse is fit they can compete as and when they like. This is not a good idea because the horse needs time to recover and rest after competing. The horse is worked hard at a show and in some cases the horse's body is pushed to the limits. This can exhaust a horse and their legs may become swollen and their muscles tired and achy. For this reason the horse should be allowed 2-3 days to recover and should only be competed again once they seem to be going well without any physical problems. If the horse is unsound, not fit or is unwell for some reason they should not be taken to the show.

If the horse has recently been given a vaccination e.g. for equine influenza, they should not be worked for 3-4 days and not taken to a show for 1 week. This allows the horse's body to get back to normal after their jab so they feel fit and healthy again.

When horse or rider are not prepared or they are not yet working well together **(Fig. 118)** or achieving what needs to be achieved in order to compete successfully they should avoid competing until their goals have been reached and both horse and rider are ready for showing.

Figure 118: This horse and rider were not working together properly which led to miscommunication and a fall.

There is nothing actually stopping the horse or rider competing (providing they have qualified to enter if the competition is affiliated) but if the horse or rider is not prepared for the show it could be a waste of money as there is usually an entry fee.

Other factors to bare in mind when considering taking a horse to a show are ground and weather conditions. If the ground is particularly hard it can damage the horse's feet and if the ground is really wet or muddy it could affect the horse's balance and the risk of accidents is greater. The weather can affect the ground conditions greatly so be sure to check the weather forecast in advance. Bad weather such as strong wind, heavy rain, hail or snow can distract the horse and even scare them which can cause the horse to stop listening to the rider or spooking and causing an accident. Not only that but it is unpleasant for both horse and rider so think about this beforehand!

How to get the Horse Fit for Competing

There are numerous ways to prepare the horse for competing and you can mix and match any methods that work best for you and the horse.

⋏ Put the horse on the walker **(Fig. 119)** 6 days per week for about 45 minutes at an active walk. This can even be increased to a trot (after they have warmed up) if the horse is fit and used to the walker but do keep an eye on the horse while doing this to make sure they are not getting too tired. Perhaps start them trotting for 10 minutes and gradually increase the time as you see them getting fitter.

Figure 119: A modern horse walker. Horses can walk loose in their section or if they keep stopping or try to turn around they can be tied to the barrier in front of them. Modern day walkers will stop if it encounters an obstruction. When horses realise this they may do it on purpose!

⅄ Hack the horse out regularly as this will strengthen their legs and keep their interest. Try some simple transitions and exercises to keep the horse switched on.

⅄ Lunge the horse for around 20 minutes several times a week to school and exercise the horse **(Fig. 120)**.

⅄ Ride the horse several times per week to school and exercise. Fit in as much practice as

Figure 120: Lunging the horse in both directions exercises the horse and gives the handler a chance to work on transitions.

possible so both you and the horse benefit and improve together.

⅄ If several horses are going to the show and you do not have enough time to exercise each one individually ride one and lead another at the same time. This is only really suitable for exercise purposes as you cannot offer much in the way of instruction to the horse you are leading other than using your voice. Be sure to alternate which horse you ride and which horse you lead so you get a feel for how each horse is going. This way they all get some degree of schooling too.

⅄ Unless it is really necessary to keep the horse stabled, turn them out as much as possible. This allows their mind to wind down so they can act more naturally and they also have the freedom of movement which will help to prevent them stiffening up which may happen if they are cooped up in a stable. They also have the opportunity to get more exercise should they decide to charge around the field!

⚑ And finally – allow 2-3 months to get the horse fit and schooled for the show (preparation time depends on how advanced the class is). Horses that are competing at the highest levels should ideally be kept fit all year round whereas horses that are taken to local weekend shows tend to take some time off and are exercised and schooled nearer the time.

Paperwork

If you are considering taking a horse to a show, whether they are your own or they belong to a yard, you may need to take some paperwork with you. This is not always the case. Unaffiliated shows may not require you to bring paperwork with you but affiliated shows will.

Firstly, the rider or owner of the horse needs to be a member of the governing body e.g. BSJA (British Show Jumping Association) and the horse will need to be registered with them also. For affiliated shows and some unaffiliated shows an entry form for the show should have been filled in several weeks prior to the show and sent in.

On arrival, you may need to present an up to date certificate of your horse's vaccinations, mainly to show the horse has been vaccinated against tetanus and equine influenza. This certificate can usually be found in the horse's passport – this will also need to be taken to the competition. You will need to show proof of rider or owner membership and the horse's registration documents. You should also have been sent information about your start times for competing and it is best to bring this with you to remind yourself what time you need to ride. If you have not been sent information about the competition schedule you should ring the show office in plenty of time to find out what time you are riding. This is particularly important for dressage and event riders as these times are usually very exact.

THE EQUINE
THEORY TEST

Stable

Management

Typical Yard Duties

Task 1

Create a timetable for the routine on your yard. If you don't have your own horse or work on a yard, make one up!

Time	Task

What can you do if you have finished all of your jobs but other people on the yard are still working?

_____

_____

_____

_____

_____

_____

Task 2

Name 3 methods for mucking out stables and give a brief explanation of what is involved for each one.

Method 1: _____

_____

_____

_____

_____

Method 2: _____

_____

_____

_____

_____

Method 3: _____

_____

_____

_____

_____

If a horse is in the stable when you come to muck out where and how would you secure them?

_____

_____

_____

_____

_____

What should you always tie the horse to if you are tying them to a securing ring or another sturdy object?

_____

_____

Task 3

Give two methods for disposing of muck. Briefly explain how you would do each.

Method 1: _____

_____

_____

_____

_____

_____

Method 2: _____

_____

_____

_____

_____

Storage Buildings

Task 1

Name four types of storage building.

    1. _____

    2. _____

    3. _____

    4. _____

Explain how you would store the relevant items in each store room and how you would look after each one.

Building 1: _____

_____

_____

_____

Building 2: _____

_____

_____

_____

Building 3: _____

_____

_____

_____

Building 4: _____

_____

_____

_____

Field Care

Task 1

Name four types of shelter for a horse in the field and state what each one will adequately shelter the horse from.

1. _____

2. _____

3. _____

4. _____

List some pros and cons of a man made field shelter.

Pros:

1. _____

2. _____

3. _____

Cons:

1. _____

2. _____

3. _____

Task 2

List four ways of providing water to a horse in the field.

1. _____

2. _____

3. _____

4. _____

What type of water supply should you prevent the horse getting access to?

_____
_____
_____
_____
_____

What is the importance of a fresh and constant supply of water to the horse?

_____
_____
_____
_____
_____

Task 3

Clearing the field of horse manure on a daily basis is important for the horse's health. Why is this?

_____

_____

_____

_____

_____

Outline the best method for clearing manure from a large field. Include what tools you would use.

_____

_____

_____

_____

_____

_____

What other method can you use to help eliminate the spread of worm eggs without removing droppings from the field? How and when would you do this?

_____

_____

_____

_____

_____

_____

_____

Task 4

Create a check list that you can take out to the field on a weekly basis to fill in when inspecting the overall safety of the field, its contents and its borders.

Things to check	Satisfactory	Not Satisfactory	Notes

If a danger is spotted and cannot be easily rectified by yourself what should you do?

Winter Care

Task 1

What factors determine whether a horse should be wearing a rug or not?

_____
_____
_____
_____
_____

When applying a rug, in what order should you fasten the straps at the front, middle and rear of the rug?

1st : _____

2nd : _____

3rd : _____

When removing a rug, in what order should you unfasten the straps at the front, middle and rear of the rug?

1st : _____

2nd : _____

3rd : _____

List four things you should check a horse's body for at least twice a week when they are living out with a rug on.

   1. _____

   2. _____

   3. _____

   4. _____

List three things a rug should be checked for on a daily basis when a horse is rugged up and living out.

   1. _____

   2. _____

   3. _____

Task 2

How often should you check the horse's water supply in freezing conditions?

_____

Give some examples of how to help prevent the horse's water supply freezing up.

_____

_____

_____

_____

Task 3

Why do horses sometimes need access to hay when they are in a field during winter?

_____

_____

_____

_____

_____

How would you distribute the hay safely in a field with several horses present?

_____

_____

_____

_____

_____

Task 4

If you decide to increase or change your horse's feed to help keep them warm during winter what is the best way to go about doing this safely?

_____

_____

_____

_____

_____

How can changing a horse's diet too quickly effect the horse and why?

_____

_____

_____

_____

_____

_____

Give two methods for feeding a group of horses in the field.

Method 1: _____

_____

_____

_____

_____

Method 2: _____

_____

_____

_____

How would you feed a group of horses in the field if one or more of the horses had medication in their feed?

_____

_____

_____

_____

_____

_____

The Grass Kept Horse

Task 1

Create a check list of things to do and look for in the field and on the horse on a daily basis.

Checking The Field	Checked / Amended?	Notes
Checking the Horse	**Checked / Amended?**	**Notes**

Task 2

Describe a safe method for releasing a horse into the field.

_____

_____

_____

_____

_____

_____

_____

Describe a safe method for a group of people releasing horses into the field at the same time.

_____

_____

_____

_____

_____

_____

_____

Describe a safe method for bringing in a horse from the field.

_____

_____

_____

_____

_____

_____

_____

If you are bringing in a field of horses and there are now only two left in the field, what could happen when you bring in the next horse and one is left in the field?

_____
_____
_____
_____
_____
_____
_____
_____

How can you prevent this from happening?

_____
_____
_____
_____
_____
_____
_____

Feeding

Task 1

Name three categories of feed and give an example of each.

1. _____

2. _____

3. _____

Task 2

Create your own feed chart.

Explain the importance of good hygiene when preparing feeds.

_____
_____
_____

List some methods of giving a feed to a stabled horse.

1. _____

2. _____

3. _____

Task 3

List some methods of giving hay to a stabled horse.

1. _____

2. _____

3. _____

What would you do to the hay prior to giving it if a horse has dust allergies?

_____
_____

What roughage could you give to a horse that required more energy?

_____

Task 4

When should water be provided to a stabled horse?

_____

_____

_____

_____

_____

Give two methods for providing water to a stabled horse.

Method 1: _____

Method 2: _____

How often should both of these containers of water be cleaned out?

_____

_____

_____

_____

_____

Going Further

The Stable

Task 1

Fill in the correct measurements in the empty boxes.

Size of Horse	Size of Stable
Ponies and up to 15hh	' X ' (. m X . m)
Horses above 15hh	' X ' (. m X . m)
Large or heavy horses	' X ' (. m X . m)
Foaling box	' X ' (. m X . m)
Other Measurements	
Kick boards	'(. m) high
Height up to eaves	'(. m) high
Bottom door	'(. m) high
Top door	'(. m) high
Door width	'(. m) wide

Why is it important for a horse to be in a stable that is the correct size for them?

_____

_____
_____

Task 2

List four methods for helping to keep a stable fresh and airy.

1. _____

2. _____

3. _____

4. _____

Give three materials a stable could be built from. Give the pros and cons of each.

Material 1: _____

Pros: _____
           _____
           _____

Cons: _____
           _____
           _____

Material 2: _____

Pros: _____
           _____
           _____

Cons: _____
           _____
           _____

Material 3: _____

Pros: _____
           _____
           _____

Cons: _____
           _____
           _____

Task 3

Draw some stable fittings and accessories onto the diagram below. Place them where you think they would be sensibly positioned. Label your diagram so you know what each item is.

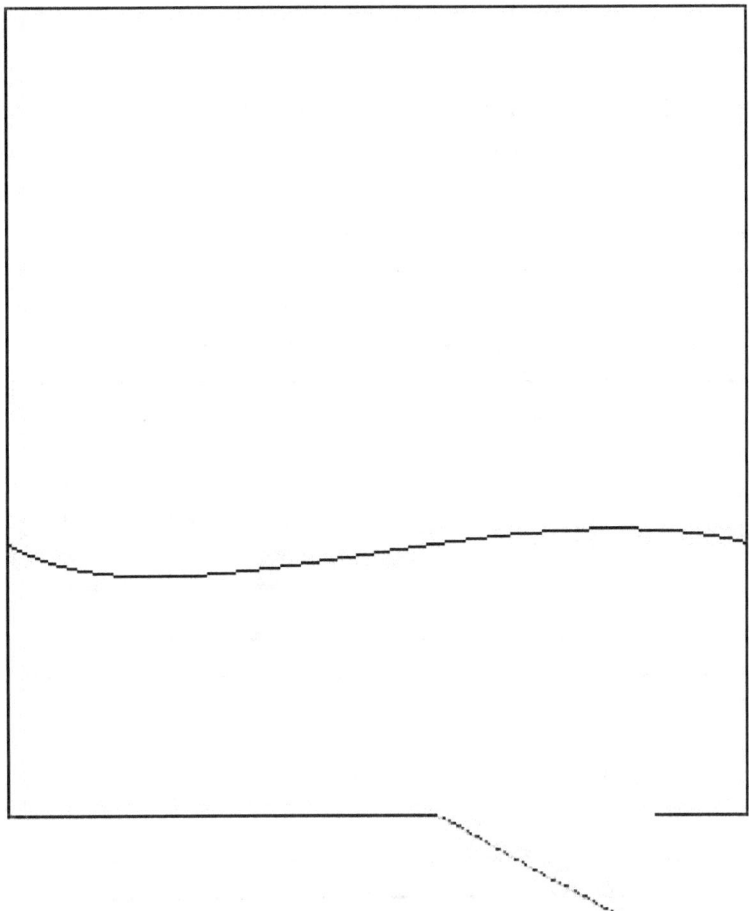

Task 4

Why should the floor of a stable be angled slightly so that it slopes down towards the back end?

_____

_____

How can the layout of the stables help to prevent a horse developing stable vices?

_____

_____

_____

_____

_____

_____

Where should light switches, lights and sockets be placed on the outside of the stable?

_____

_____

What is the purpose of an overhang?

_____

_____

_____

_____

_____

_____

Bedding

Task 1

Name three places where bedding can be used.

1. _____

2. _____

3. _____

What is the purpose of bedding?

_____
_____
_____

Name five different types of bedding and give the pros and cons of each.

Type 1: _____

Pros: _____
_____
_____

Cons: _____
_____
_____

Type 2: _____

Pros: _____
_____
_____

Cons: _____
_____
_____

Type 3: _____
Pros: _____
_____
_____

Cons: _____
_____
_____

Type 4: _____
Pros: _____
_____
_____

Cons: _____
_____
_____

Type 5: _____

Pros: _____

_____

_____

Cons: _____

_____

_____

Environmental Considerations

Task 1

Before you can carry out any building work what must you do beforehand and how would you go about doing this?

_____
_____
_____
_____
_____
_____
_____

Task 2

Imagine you are about to build a yard from scratch. Describe what materials you would use to build the stables and their immediate surroundings. Explain how using these materials could help the environment or economy and how they can help you to create a low maintenance yard.

_____
_____
_____
_____
_____
_____
_____
_____

_____

_____

_____

_____

_____

_____

_____

_____

_____

_____

_____

_____

_____

_____

_____

Task 3

List some things you should take into consideration when the yard has neighbours.

A _____

A _____

A _____

A _____

A _____

A _____

Task 4

How can you make the yard more energy efficient?

_____

_____

_____

_____

_____

_____

_____

_____

_____

_____

_____

_____

Field Care

Task 1

Roughly how much land should be available for each horse?

_____

What could you do in the winter if the horses are turned out and there is not enough grass for them to graze on?

_____

_____

Task 2

Name three types of acceptable fencing for a field of horses and explain why each one is a good choice.

Fence 1: _____

Fence 2: _____

Fence 3: _____

Name two types of unacceptable fencing for a field of horses and explain why each one is a poor choice.

Fence 1: _____

Fence 2: _____

Task 3

What dangers can a muddy gateway cause?

_____

_____

_____

_____

_____

_____

_____

_____

How can you prevent a gateway from becoming muddy?

_____

_____

_____

_____

_____

_____

_____

_____

_____

_____

_____

_____

Task 4

How is a field shelter beneficial to a horse?

_____
_____
_____
_____
_____

What could happen to the horse if they had no shelter in the field?

_____
_____
_____
_____
_____
_____
_____

Give a rough specification of a man made field shelter.

_____
_____
_____
_____
_____
_____
_____

Task 5

Give two methods for clearing the field of weeds and unwanted plants.

Method 1: _____

Method 2: _____

If there is only one field available how could you make sure there is always plenty of well grown fresh grass available?

_____
_____
_____
_____
_____

Some horses (ponies in particular) develop laminitis. In what way could the grass be a cause of this?

_____
_____
_____
_____

How could you turn a laminitic horse out and prevent them from grazing too much therefore making their condition worse?

_____
_____
_____
_____
_____

Dangerous Plants

Task 1

Give a method for checking a large field for dangerous plants.

_____

_____

_____

_____

_____

How could you go about removing the dangerous plants?

_____

_____

_____

How should you dispose of dangerous plants?

_____

_____

_____

What health and safety precautions should you take when handling dangerous plants?

_____

_____

_____

_____

How can you prevent a horse getting to the dangerous plants if it is not possible to remove them?

_____

_____

Task 2

What should you do if you suspect a horse has ingested a dangerous plant?

_____

_____

List nine plants that are toxic to horses.

1. _____

2. _____

3. _____

4. _____

5. _____

6. _____

7. _____

8. _____

9. _____

List some common symptoms a horse may show as a result of ingesting toxic plants.

➤ _____

➤ _____

➤ _____

➤ _____

➤ _____

➤ _____

➤ _____

➤ _____

➤ _____

Feeding

Task 1

State whether the following are roughage, succulents or concentrates:

Alfalfa

Apples

Beans

Carrots

Chaff

Cooked barley

Crushed barley

Flaked maize

Grass

Hay

Haylage

Naked oats

Peas

Rolled oats

Sugar beet

Task 2

List 10 rules of good feeding.

1. _____

2. _____

3. _____

4. _____

5. _____

6. _____

7. _____

8. _____

9. _____

10. _____

Task 3

What factors determine how much feed to give a horse?

_____
_____
_____
_____
_____
_____
_____
_____
_____
_____

Task 4

Give an example of an accurate method for working out how much feed to give a horse on a daily basis.

_____

_____

_____

_____

_____

Give an example of a less accurate method for working out how much feed to give a horse on a daily basis.

_____

_____

_____

_____

Using your calculations from one of your examples you have provided above, show how you would work out how to divide the total feed per day into roughage and concentrates.

_____

_____

_____

_____

_____

_____

_____

_____

_____

Task 5

Describe how to make a bran mash.

_____

_____

_____

_____

_____

_____

_____

_____

_____

_____

_____

Outline a safe method for administering medicines in feeds.

_____

_____

_____

_____

_____

_____

Showing

Tack

Task 1

Label the diagrams:

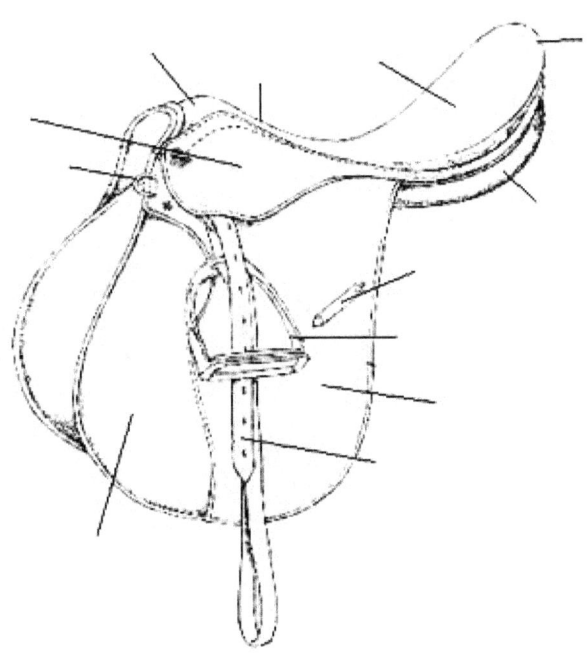

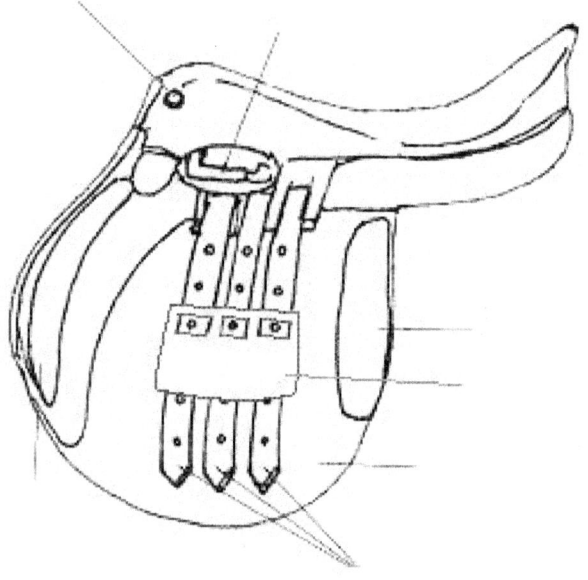

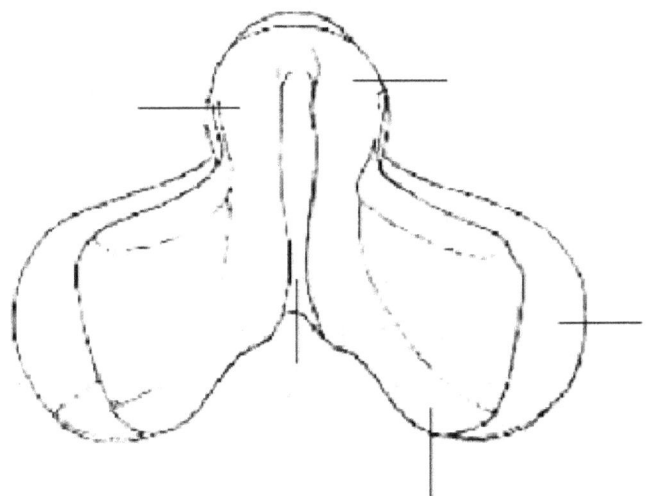

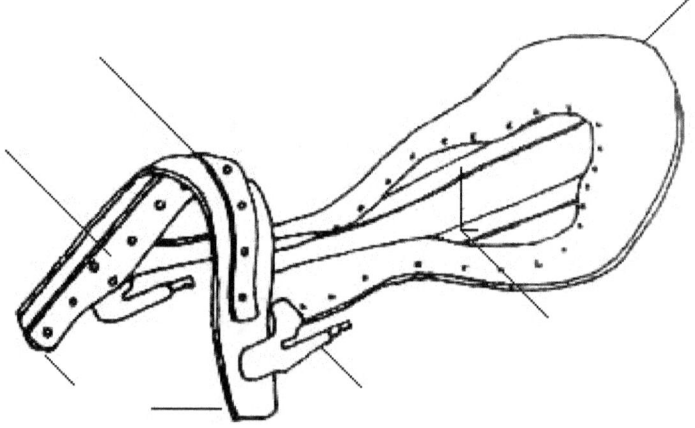

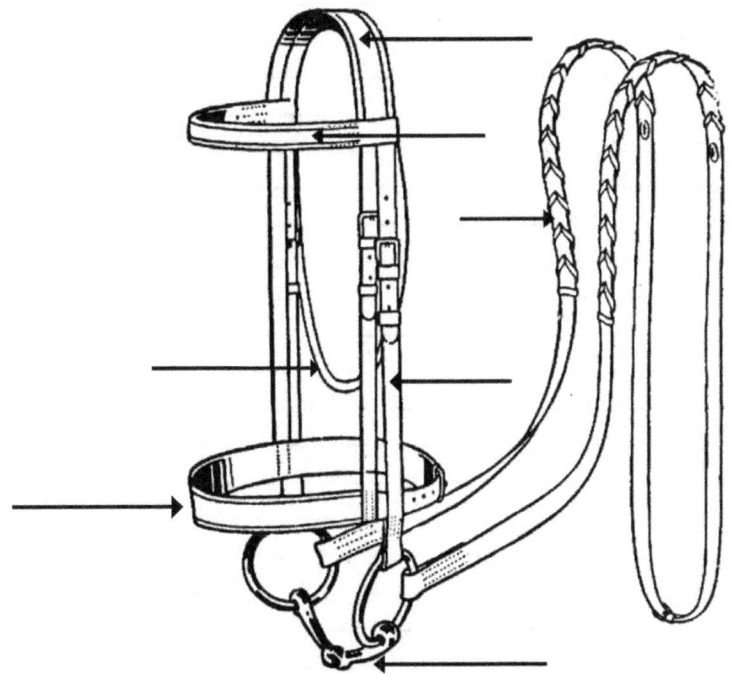

Task 2

Explain how you would tack up a horse using a snaffle bridle and a general purpose saddle.

_____

_____

_____

_____

_____

_____

_____

_____

_____

_____

_____

_____

_____

_____

_____

_____

_____

_____

_____

_____

_____

_____

_____

_____

Explain how you would untack a horse after a session of hard work.

_____
_____
_____
_____
_____
_____
_____
_____
_____
_____
_____
_____
_____
_____
_____
_____
_____

Task 3

Why is it important to keep tack clean?

_____
_____
_____
_____
_____
_____

How often should you clean tack?

_____

_____

_____

Explain how you should clean your tack after a ride.

_____

_____

_____

_____

_____

_____

_____

_____

_____

_____

_____

_____

How should you store tack?

_____

_____

_____

_____

_____

_____

Preparing the Horse

Task 1

List the items you need to carry out a thorough groom.

➤ _____

➤ _____

➤ _____

➤ _____

➤ _____

➤ _____

➤ _____

➤ _____

➤ _____

➤ _____

➤ _____

➤ _____

➤ _____

➤ _____

➤ _____

➤ _____

Why is it important to groom a horse on a regular basis?

_____

_____

_____

_____

_____

Why is it important to groom a horse for a show?

_____

_____

_____

_____

_____

Task 2

Write a step by step guide on how to give a horse a thorough groom.

Step 1: _____

Step 2: _____

Step 3: _____

Step 4: _____

Step 5: _____

Step 6: _____

Step 7: _____

Step 8: _____

Step 9: _____

Step 10: _____

Step 11: _____

Step 12: _____

Step 13: _____

Step 14: _____

Step 15: _____

Step 16: _____

Step 17: _____

Step 18: _____

Step 19: _____

Step 20: _____

Write a step by step guide on how to apply a tail bandage.

Step 1: _____

Step 2: _____

Step 3: _____

Step 4: _____

Step 5: _____

How should you remove a tail bandage?

_____
_____
_____
_____
_____

Write a step by step guide on how to plait a mane using rubber bands.

Step 1: _____

Step 2: _____

Step 3: _____

Step 4: _____

Step 5: _____

Give some examples of how to keep a grooming kit clean and how to avoid the spread of infections.

_____
_____
_____
_____
_____
_____
_____
_____

Task 3

What items will you need to bath a horse?

- _____

- _____

- _____

- _____

- _____

- _____

- _____

- _____

Why is it important to tie the horse up with a loose quick release knot while bathing?

_____
_____
_____
_____
_____
_____
_____
_____
_____

Write a step by step guide on how to bath a horse.

Step 1: _____

Step 2: _____

Step 3: _____

Step 4: _____

Step 5: _____

Step 6: _____

Step 7: _____

Step 8: _____

Step 9: _____

Step 10: _____

Step 11: _____

Step 12: _____

Step 13: _____

Step 14: _____

Step 15: _____

Task 4

How can you help to prevent the horse getting dirty overnight if they are bathed the day before a show?

_____
_____
_____
_____
_____
_____
_____

Write a step by step guide on how to apply stable bandages.

Step 1: _____

Step 2: _____

Step 3: _____

Step 4: _____

Step 5: _____

Step 6: _____

Step 7: _____

Step 8: _____

Step 9: _____

Step 10: _____

How should you remove stable bandages?

_____

_____

_____

_____

_____

_____

What are the benefits of using stable bandages?

_____

_____

_____

_____

_____

_____

_____

What is the difference between a stable bandage and a polo wrap?
When and why would a polo wrap be used?

_____

_____

_____

_____

_____

_____

_____

The Role of the Groom

Task 1

Make a list of things you should do the day before travelling to the show.

➤ _____

➤ _____

➤ _____

➤ _____

➤ _____

➤ _____

➤ _____

➤ _____

➤ _____

➤ _____

➤ _____

➤ _____

➤ _____

➤ _____

➤ _____

Make a list of things you should do on the morning of the show.

- _____
- _____
- _____
- _____
- _____
- _____
- _____
- _____
- _____
- _____

Make a list of things to put in the lorry before travelling to the show.

- _____
- _____
- _____
- _____
- _____
- _____
- _____
- _____
- _____
- _____
- _____

Make a list of things you should do to help your rider while at the show.

- _____
- _____
- _____
- _____
- _____
- _____
- _____
- _____
- _____
- _____
- _____
- _____
- _____
- _____
- _____

Make a list of things you should do after the show once you have returned home.

- _____
- _____
- _____
- _____
- _____
- _____

Types of Competitions

Task 1

Name 7 disciplines that can all be competed in and briefly describe what each one involves.

1.

2.

3.

4.

5.

6.

7.

Transportation

Task 1

List 3 types of equine transportation.

1. _____

2. _____

3. _____

Why should you be especially careful when buying second hand transportation?

_____

_____

_____

_____

_____

_____

_____

Make a check list you can use for checking the safety of the equine transportation before it is used or bought.

Checking The Transportation	Satisfactory?	Notes

Make a check list you can use for doing vehicle checks to make sure the transport or towing vehicle is road worthy.

Checking The Vehicle	Satisfactory?	Notes

Task 2

List some ways to help keep a horse comfortable during transportation.

- _____

- _____

- _____

- _____

- _____

- _____

- _____

- _____

- _____

- _____

What type of roads should be avoided if possible when transporting horses and why?

_____
_____
_____
_____
_____
_____
_____

Which roads are best for transporting horses on and why?

_____

_____

_____

_____

_____

_____

Give three methods for planning your route. Give the pros and cons for each.

Method 1: _____

Pros: _____

_____

Cons: _____

_____

Method 2: _____

Pros: _____

_____

Cons: _____

_____

Method 3: _____

Pros: _____

_____

Cons: _____

_____

Task 3

What is the reason for putting travel clothing on the horse?

_____

_____

_____

_____

_____

Explain how each item listed below helps to protect the horse during transit.

Poll Guard

_____

_____

_____

_____

Rug

_____

_____

_____

Tail Guard

_____

_____

_____

_____

Travel Boots

_____
_____
_____
_____
_____

Over Reach Boots

_____
_____
_____
_____

Why should a leather head collar be used instead of a nylon one when transporting horses?

_____
_____
_____

Name some rugs that are suitable for travelling in. Give the pros and cons of each.

Rug 1:   _____

Pros: _____

                _____

Cons: _____

                _____

Rug 2: _____

Pros: _____
_____

Cons: _____
_____

Rug 3: _____

Pros: _____
_____

Cons: _____
_____

Rug 4: _____

Pros: _____
_____

Cons: _____
_____

Rug 5: _____

Pros: _____
_____

Cons: _____
_____

What can be used to protect the tail instead of a tail guard?

_____

What can be used to protect the legs in place of travel boots? Give the pros and cons of each.

Item 1: _____

Pros: _____

_____

Cons: _____

_____

Item 2: _____

Pros: _____

_____

Cons: _____

_____

Item 3: _____

Pros: _____

_____

Cons: _____

_____

What could you use to secure the rug(s) in place instead of surcingles?

_____

<u>Going Further</u>

Tack

Task 1

List four types of saddles commonly used in the UK. Give a brief explanation of how the shape of the saddle aids the rider.

1.

2.

3.

4.

Task 2

List five types of bridle commonly used in the UK. Give a brief explanation of how the action of each bridle aids the rider.

1.

2.

3.

4.

5.

Task 3

List six types of noseband commonly used in the UK. Give a brief explanation of the action of each noseband.

1.

2.

3.

4.

5.

6.

Which noseband is the most common and gentle?

_____

Task 4

Fill in the table below giving a brief explanation of what each item does or action it provides.

Name of Bit	**Affect on Horse**

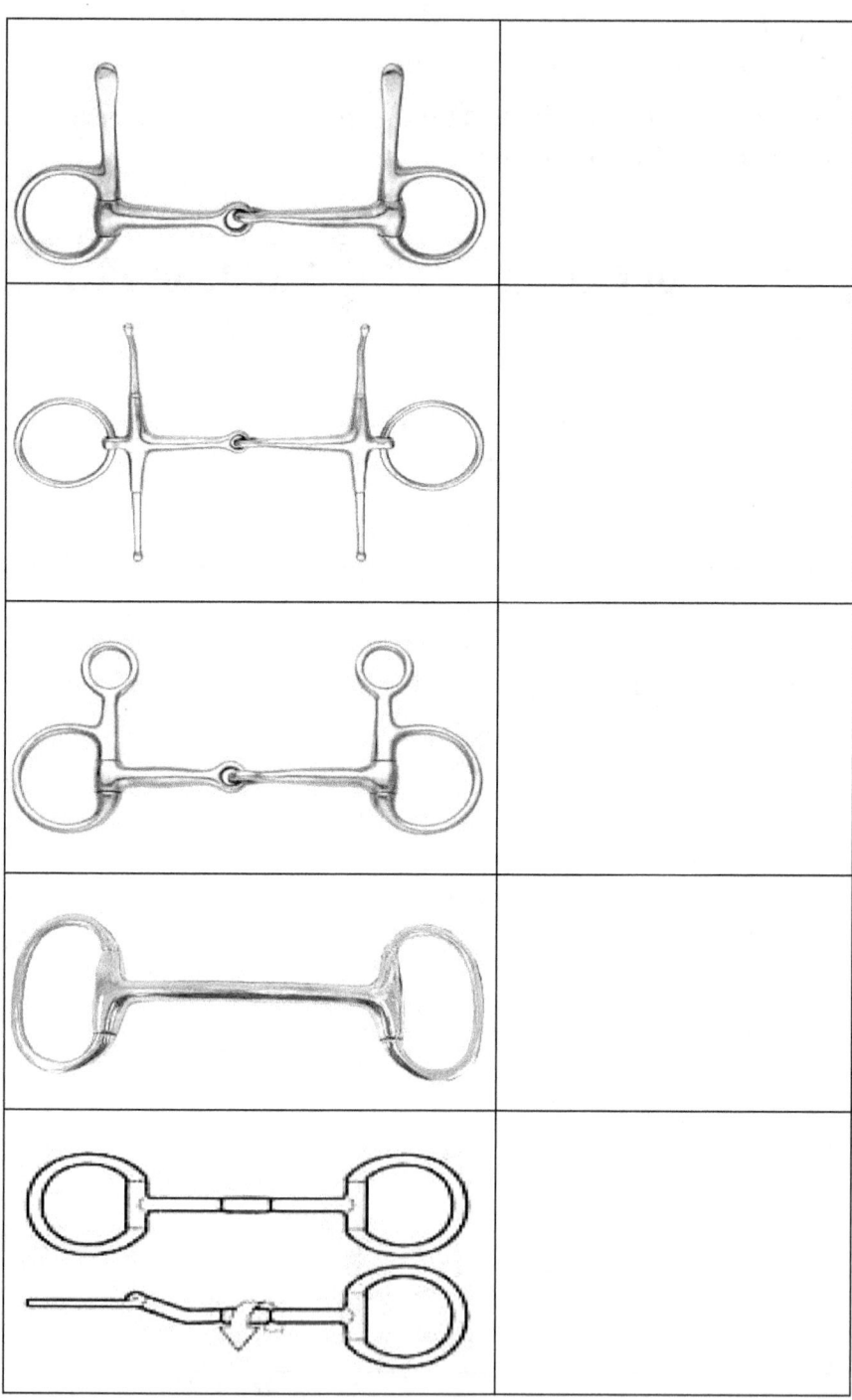

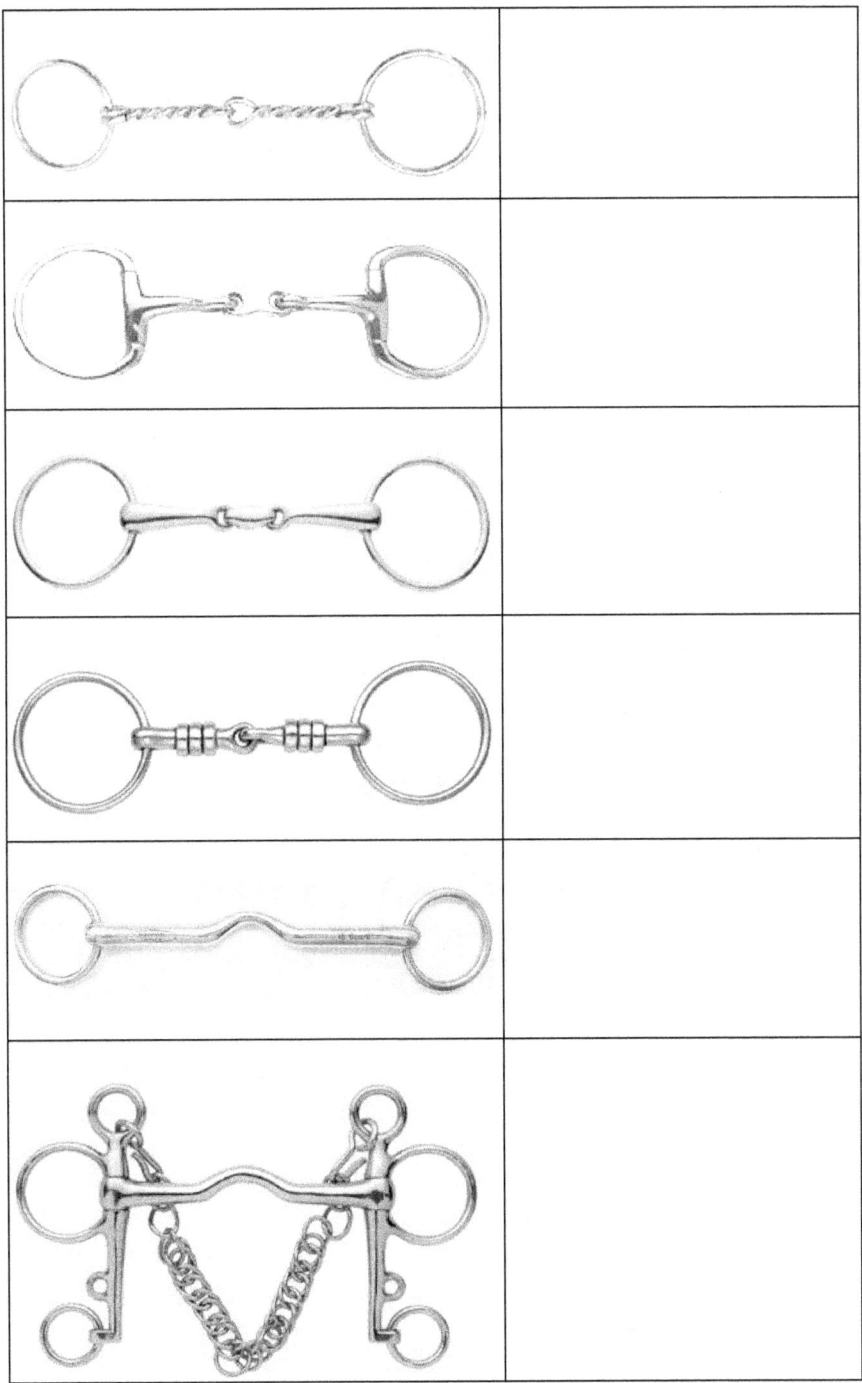

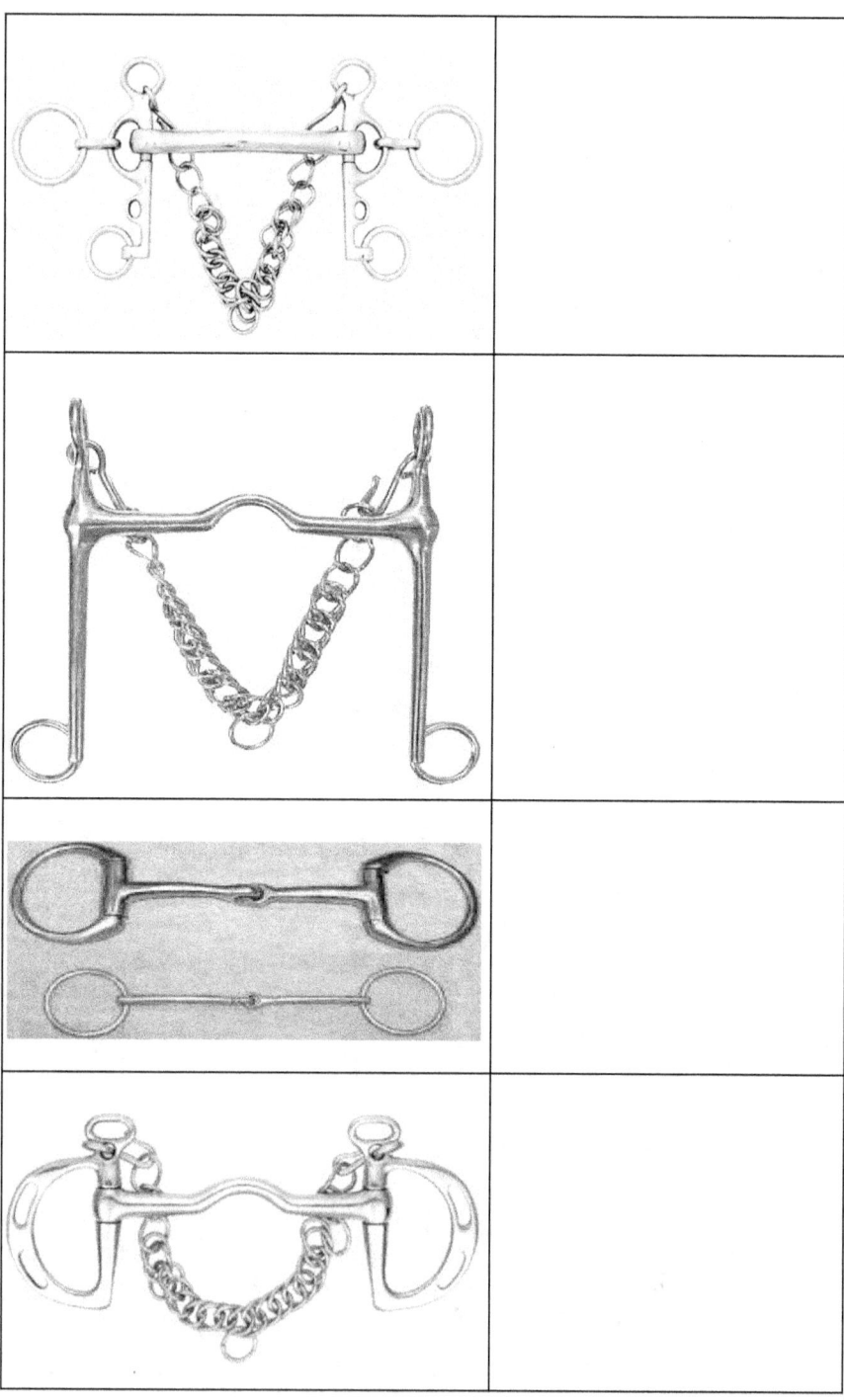

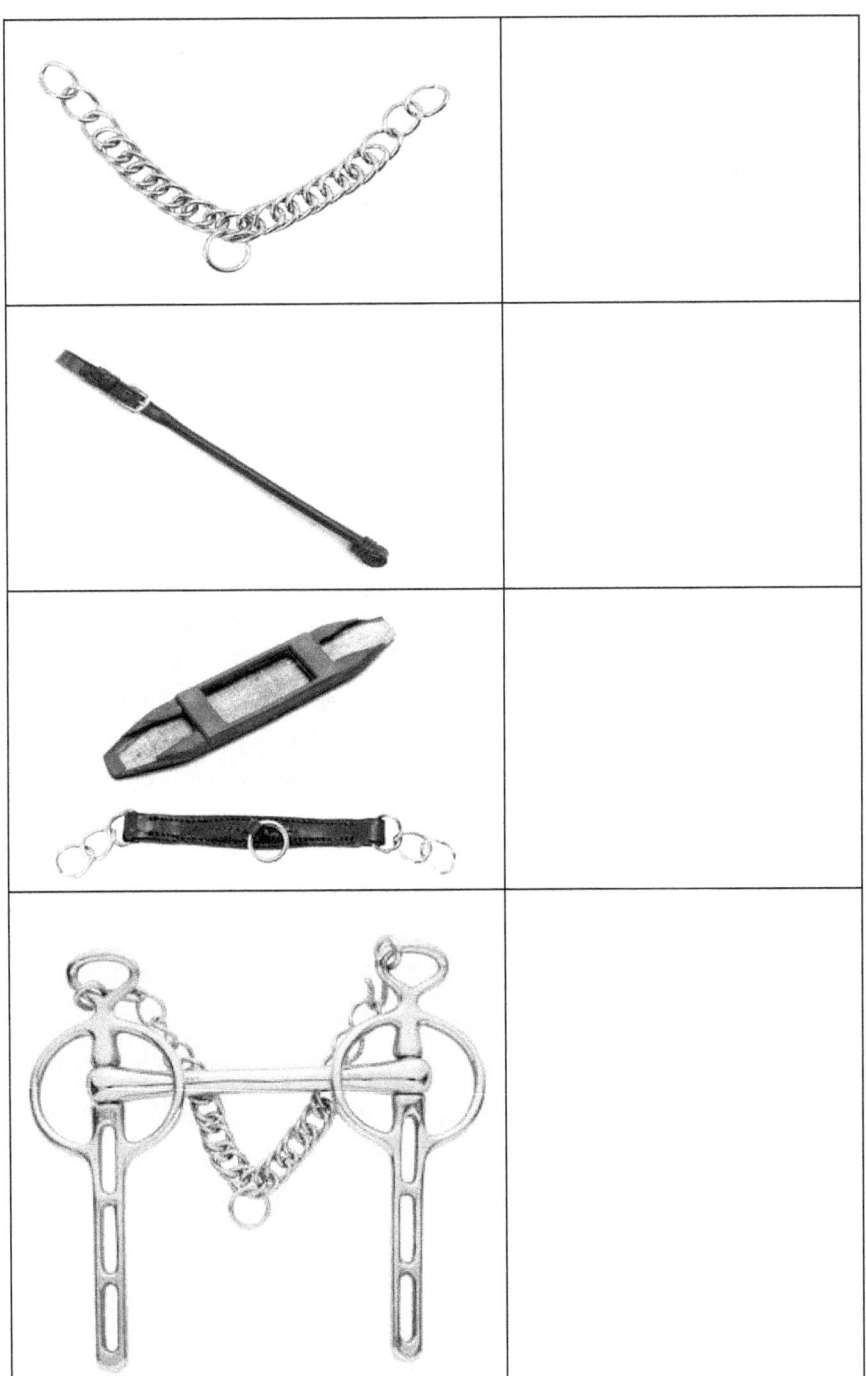

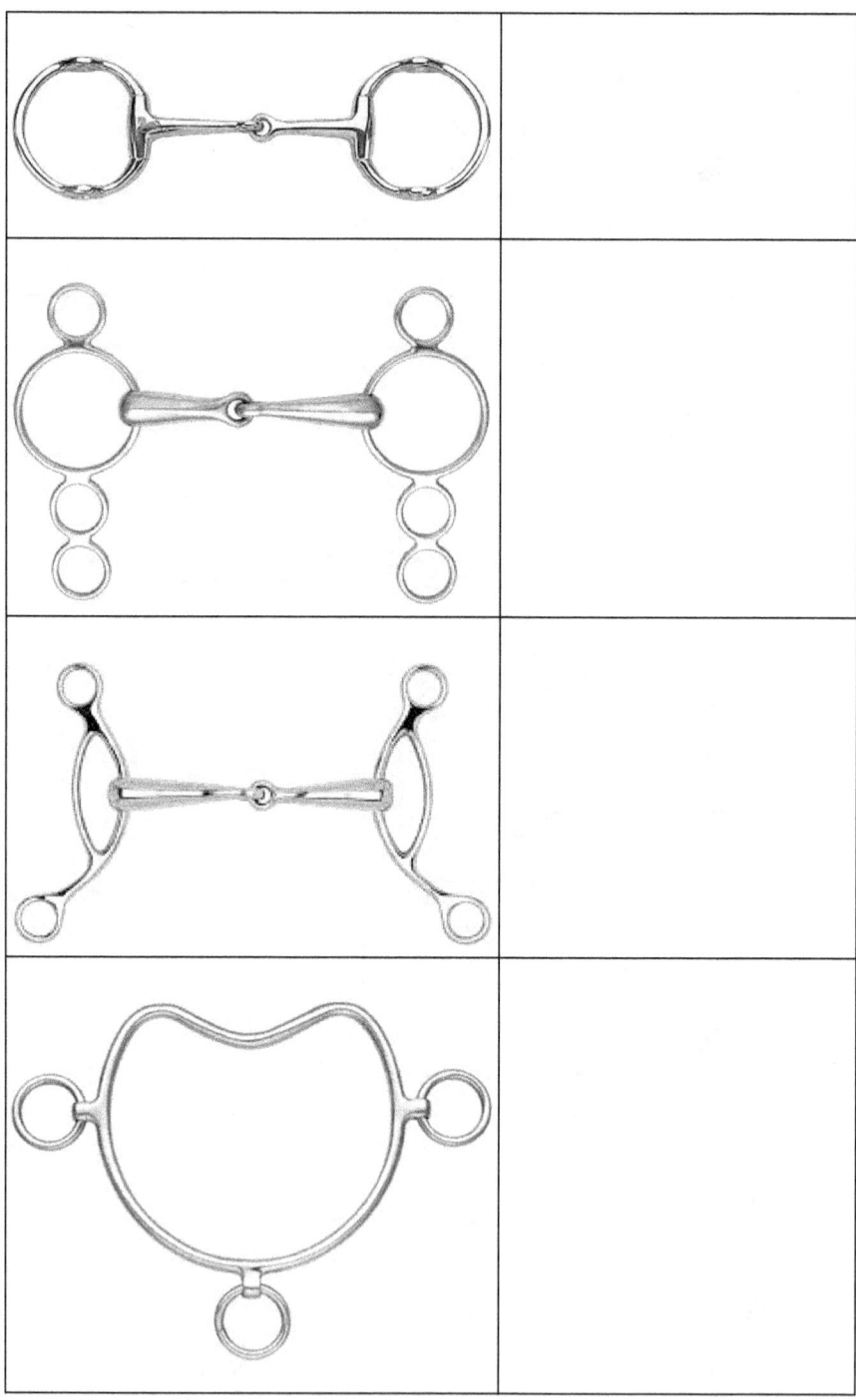

Task 5

List 12 types of bit material.

1. _____

2. _____

3. _____

4. _____

5. _____

6. _____

7. _____

8. _____

9. _____

10. _____

11. _____

12. _____

Competition Grooming

Task 1

When and why would a horse need clipping?

_____
_____
_____
_____
_____
_____
_____

List some things you will need to clip a horse.

⅄ _____

⅄ _____

⅄ _____

⅄ _____

⅄ _____

⅄ _____

⅄ _____

Write a step by step guide on how to clip a horse.

Step 1: _____

Step 2: _____

Step 3: _____

Step 4: _____

Step 5: _____

Step 6: _____

Step 7: _____

Step 8: _____

Step 9: _____

Step 10:_____

How could you distract a nervous horse while clipping?

_____

_____

_____

_____

_____

_____

_____

_____

List six styles of clip.

1. _____

2. _____

3. _____

4. _____

5. _____

6. _____

How could you check your clipping is even and the same on both sides?

_____
_____
_____
_____
_____
_____

What should you do when you have finished clipping the horse?

_____
_____
_____
_____
_____
_____
_____

Task 2

What areas of the horse can be trimmed?

_____
_____
_____
_____

When should a horse not be trimmed?

_____
_____
_____

Explain how you would trim a horse's legs.

_____
_____
_____
_____
_____

Write a step by step guide on how to trim a horse's tail.

Step 1: _____

Step 2: _____

Step 3: _____

Step 4: _____

Step 5: _____

Explain how you would trim a horse's head and ears.

_____

_____

_____

_____

_____

Explain how you would trim a horse's mane and forelock if it could not be pulled.

_____

_____

_____

_____

Task 3

Why is it better to pull a mane rather than trim it?

_____

_____

_____

_____

When is the best time to pull a mane?

_____

_____

_____

Write a step by step guide on how to pull a horse's mane.

Step 1: _____

Step 2: _____

Step 3: _____

Step 4: _____

Step 5: _____

Write a step by step guide on how to pull a horse's tail.

Step 1: _____

Step 2: _____

Step 3: _____

Step 4: _____

Step 5: _____

What could you do to assess how a horse might react to having their mane or tail pulled if you have not seen them have it done before?

_____

_____

_____

_____

_____

What PPE could you wear to protect yourself when you are pulling the mane or tail of a horse you are unsure about?

_____

_____

_____

Task 4

Give two examples of when you might plait a horse's mane (rolled up plaits).

Example 1: _____

Example 2: _____

What tools do you need to plait a horse with a needle and thread?

➤ _____

➤ _____

➤ _____

➤ _____

➤ _____

➤ _____

➤ _____

➤ _____

Write a step by step guide on how to plait a horse's mane with a needle and thread.

Step 1: _____

Step 2: _____

Step 3: _____

Step 4: _____

Step 5: _____

Step 6: _____

Step 7: _____

Step 8: _____

Step 9: _____

Step 10: _____

Step 11: _____

Step 12: _____

What type of plait is commonly put in the tail and sometimes the forelock?

_____

Bathing Methods

Task 1

List three methods of bathing a horse and briefly describe how to do each.

1.

2.

3.

Task 2

Why might you need to restrain a horse?

_____
_____
_____
_____
_____
_____
_____

List 4 methods of restraining a horse.

1. _____

2. _____

3. _____

4. _____

Transportation

Task 1

List four legal requirements which must be adhered to before taking any form of transport onto the road.

1. _____

2. _____

3. _____

4. _____

Why is it important to make sure all four of these legal requirements are met?

_____
_____
_____
_____
_____

Task 2

List three weight limits that should not be exceeded for legal and safety purposes.

1. _____

2. _____

3. _____

Why is it important not to exceed maximum weight limits?

_____

_____

_____

_____

Task 3

When are you legally obliged to install a tachograph into your equine transportation or towing vehicle?

_____

_____

When and where should a tachograph be inspected?

_____

_____

When and where should a tachograph be recalibrated?

_____

_____

What is the purpose of a tachograph?

_____

_____

_____

_____

Task 4

List five things that can make driving a larger vehicle more challenging when transporting horses.

1. _____

2. _____

3. _____

4. _____

5. _____

Describe the safest way to pull away and come to a stop while transporting horses.

_____

_____

_____

_____

_____

_____

_____

_____

What is a safe and steady speed to travel at while transporting horses down main roads (unless signs state otherwise)?

_____

How can twisty lanes and roads with lots of roundabouts and
traffic lights affect the horse?

_____
_____
_____
_____

What times of the day are best for transporting horses and why?

_____
_____
_____
_____

Why are dual carriageways and motorways safer to transport
horses on?

_____
_____
_____
_____

What should you do if you pull the equine transportation into the
hard shoulder?

_____
_____
_____
_____

Task 5

What PPE should you wear when loading or unloading horses?

➤ _____

➤ _____

➤ _____

Why is it safer to have someone helping you load or unload horses?

_____
_____
_____
_____
_____
_____
_____

Write a step by step guide on how to load a horse into a trailer.

Step 1: _____

Step 2: _____

Step 3: _____

Step 4: _____

Step 5: _____

Write a step by step guide on how to load a horse into a horse box / lorry.

Step 1: _____

Step 2: _____

Step 3: _____

Step 4: _____

Step 5: _____

Describe the best way to lift and secure shut a ramp to a horse box / lorry.

_____
_____
_____
_____
_____
_____
_____

Why is it important to still be wearing PPE while lifting and securing shut the ramp?

_____
_____
_____
_____
_____

Which side of a trailer is best to load the horse into if only one horse is travelling?

_____

Write a step by step guide on how to unload a horse from a trailer.

Step 1: _____

Step 2: _____

Step 3: _____

Step 4: _____

Step 5: _____

Write a step by step guide on how to unload a horse from a horse box/lorry.

Step 1: _____

Step 2: _____

Step 3: _____

Step 4: _____

Step 5: _____

What should you do after unloading the horse(s)?

_____

_____

_____

_____

_____

Briefly outline seven methods for encouraging a difficult horse into a trailer or lorry.

Method 1: _____

_____

_____

_____

_____

_____

Method 2: _____

_____

_____

_____

_____

_____

Method 3: _____

_____

_____

_____

_____

_____

Method 4: _____

_____

_____

_____

_____

_____

Method 5: _____

_____

_____

_____

_____

_____

Method 6: _____

_____

_____

_____

_____

_____

Method 7: _____

_____

_____

_____

_____

_____

Why is it important to read the horse's body language while loading and unloading?

_____

_____

_____

_____

_____

Competing

Task 1

When is the best time to compete?

_____
_____
_____
_____
_____
_____
_____

How can you tell when a horse and / or rider are not ready to compete?

_____
_____
_____
_____
_____
_____

When should a horse definitely not be competed?

_____
_____
_____
_____

What other factors can determine whether you should or should not take a horse to a competition on the day?

_____

_____

_____

_____

_____

Task 2

Roughly, how long should you allow for a horse to get fit for competing?

_____

_____

_____

_____

_____

List six methods for getting a horse fit for competing.

1. _____

2. _____

3. _____

4. _____

5. _____

6. _____

Task 3

If, for example, you wanted to compete on your own horse at an affiliated show who must you register with first and who needs registering?

_____

_____

_____

_____

_____

What documentation will need to be presented at the show office before you can compete?

_____

_____

_____

_____

_____

Why is it important to have with you a schedule for the show and a note of the times you are meant to compete?

_____

_____

_____

_____

_____

_____

www.ingramcontent.com/pod-product-compliance
Lightning Source LLC
Chambersburg PA
CBHW070630290526
45790CB00001B/62